TRUMPETS FROM MONTPARNASSE

By the Same Author

THE SEVENTH MAN
A TRUE TALE OF LOVE IN TONGA
COCONUT ISLAND
JOHN GRAHAM, CONVICT
BLUE ANGELS AND WHALES
SWEET THAMES RUN SOFTLY
COMING DOWN THE WYE
LOVELY IS THE LEE
OVER THE REEFS
SWEET CORK OF THEE
COMING DOWN THE SEINE

TRUMPETS
FROM
MONTPARNASSE

by
ROBERT GIBBINGS

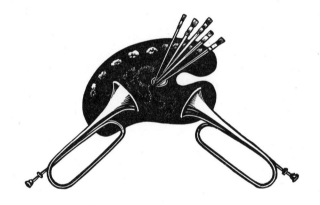

*Illustrated with eight colour plates and
forty wood engravings by the author*

NEW YORK: E. P. DUTTON & CO., INC.

TO

'JIM'

'And where are you going to this time?' asked the pilot. 'There are no bugles sounding from Mount Olympus to-day.'

'No,' I said, 'but there are trumpets calling from Montparnasse.'

Coming Down the Seine.

CHAPTER ONE

'Scarce as second-hand coffins,' commented a fellow countryman of mine when I mentioned that I was looking for a studio in Paris.

I was sitting at a café near the Lion de Belfort, at the top of the Boulevard Raspail in Montparnasse, and Henri the waiter, an old friend of mine, had introduced me to three old friends of his.

'But if you are an engraver,' said another of the three, a Frenchman, 'you have not need of a studio: a window and some light will be all that you have need of.'

'I don't want to engrave,' I said, 'I've been doing that all my life. I want to paint. I want to get away from black and white and the austerities of the graver. I want the freedom and the fun of brushes and colour.'

The third member of the trio leaned forward. He spoke English with a German accent. 'You mean,' he said, 'that you have been tight all your life and now you wish to be loose?'

'With reservations,' I replied.

'Excuse me,' he said, 'the English is not a very precise language.'

I knew that studios were as difficult to find in Paris as in London, for in one city as in the other many of them are now occupied by people who are not artists but find the simplicity of studio life an appeasement of economic distress. But I had not foreseen such a scarcity of suitable quarters. My first attempt was at an address in the Rue de Verneuil, given to me by Henri the waiter. He said that only the day before a Monsieur Franche who owned the studio had told him that as soon as it was let he was going into the country. I hopped into a taxi, but when I got to the address it was not Monsieur Franche who opened the door but a middle-aged woman wearing a paint-encrusted blue overall who said that Monsieur Franche was already in the train on his way to Collioure.

For a week after that I hunted in vain. Then I heard of an address near St Germain des Prés: 'A real studio this,' I was told, 'with a top light.' So I hurried along. The approach was through a courtyard and then up a rickety outside wooden staircase. The bell did not ring, but a knock on the door produced a short man with his front hair cut to a fringe. Yes, the studio was to let, he said, emphasizing the word studio with a gesture towards the glass roof.

It was a small room, and leaks through the framework of the glass had stained lines across the floor. I asked if the rain still came through. 'Only on wet days,' he said. This I was prepared to believe. 'But,' he added, 'there is room to fit an easel between the drips.' Of that I was not so sure.

'And there is other water laid on?' I asked.

'But naturally,' he said, 'in the court, just at the foot of the stairs.'

There was a gas-ring for cooking, and there was a mattress with some blankets which he said made a comfortable bed when unrolled. He presumed that I would be bringing my own suit-case in which to keep my clothes, because he would need the one he had for his painting materials. As the rent that he asked was enormous I postponed a decision and said that I would let him know. He bowed me to the top of the staircase and I sat down forcibly as the fourth step gave way under my weight. I decided against that proposition.

Another fruitless week went by before news came to me of a large studio in the Rue de Vaugirard, but when I got there I found that the old lady who owned it was a collector of antiques and the place was more of a museum than a workshop. She did not wish anything to be moved, except a bull terrier bitch who with three pups was asleep

3

in a large trunk. She would like them exercised each day in the garden near by.

After a month of frustration I began to think of moving to the country. Then one day in Willy Moren's studio he spoke of the Île de Ré. 'Île lumineuse,' he called it, the island of light. In the villages, he said, the houses are low and their walls are lime-washed every shade of colour and the streets are narrow and the tints get reflected from one side to the other so that you hardly know which one you are looking at. And in the country, he added, you'll see huge salt-pans covering hundreds of acres, all of them shimmering with iridescent light from the salt crystals. The salt is carried to the harbour in bright green high-wheeled carts drawn by huge straw-coloured horses, and when it is tipped down the chute into the waiting sailing ship you have to shut your eyes with the dazzlement. He spoke too of the bronzed fishermen who come ashore, with the fish scales still on their long rubber boots, to play ping-pong in the cafés, and of the fishing-boats in harbour with their nets hung out to dry, some of them blue in colour and gossamer fine for daylight fishing, others grey and of coarser mesh for night trawling. Marquet, who painted many harbours, had said of the island: 'There is no need to go further.' And then Willy added: 'Oh, I nearly forgot, the donkeys that carry the salt in panniers from the marshes to the road are dressed up in cotton trousers to protect them from the flies. Red-and-white checks are the favourite pattern. The women wear trousers too, but the

4

material is dull and the cut allows them to tuck their petti-coats inside. It gives them strange figures.'

The train to La Rochelle left the Gare Montparnasse at 9 a.m. I had arrived early and found a corner seat. Soon after I sat down, a family of four came in, heavily laden with baggage. The father, a stoutish man, pale faced but jovial, settled himself opposite to me. His suit, of a purple hue, was new and a large pearl shone in his lilac cravat. Madame his wife perched herself on the seat beside him. Her steep form was smoothly encased in black, and she wore heavy jet earrings and a large cameo brooch at her throat. The son, a weedy boy of about twelve years of age, wore baggy plus-fours reaching almost to his white ankle socks. The girl, some two years younger, thin and olive-skinned, had dark hair dragged to the top of her head and secured with two white bows before it descended in tight plaits to another pair of bows. She and her brother took the remaining window-seats. A sad-faced little man came in at the last moment and sat on my right.

The family of four were hot but happy, smiling at each other and beaming on myself and the man beside me. As the train gathered speed the mother eased her feet out of her high-heeled shoes. It was obvious that the journey was an event in their lives, and at first I thought that it was perhaps their first holiday for many years. But it turned out to be more than that. As time went on the father be-came expansive. He told me that he was on his way to Angers to take up a business that he had bought there.

He'd been a waiter all his life but he had saved enough to buy a small restaurant. 'Ah,' he said, quoting an old French proverb, 'un petit chez soi vaut mieux qu'un grand chez les autres' (a little of your own is better than a lot that belongs to others). Angers was his native town. Had I ever been there?

'Many years ago,' I said, 'I made a drawing of the castle. It had a splendid ring of towers.'

'Yes,' he said, 'seventeen towers and only two doors out of them all.' He wasn't sure but he thought that St Louis had built it against the English. Bombs had fallen on it during the last war but had damaged only the chapel inside. Had I seen the tapestries in the Bishop's Palace?

I had to admit that I hadn't even heard of them.

'Oh,' he said, 'the finest in all France.' There were about sixty of them, all depicting the Apocalypse. Never again must I miss a chance of examining them.

His thoughts went back to his restaurant. He was going to specialize in dishes of Anjou: pike with 'white butter,' eels stewed in wine, meat puddings with herbs. And he was going to have many wines of the Loire valley. Of course, everyone knew of Vouvray and Mont Louis, but he was going to have some of the lesser known ones which were charming.

I said that only the night before at La Coupole in Montparnasse I had drunk Sancerre, with Loire salmon.

'You did well,' he said. Then he looked at his watch; only two hours now before he reached Angers. He would go at once to his restaurant and take over. In three hours' time he would be the owner, *le patron*. It wasn't a very big place but it would be his own. 'Adieu, garçon!' he said, tapping himself on the chest.

The talk of food had put ideas into Madame's head. She struggled with a basket on the luggage rack and eventually got it down to the seat beside her. She took from it first a bottle of red wine which she gave to the boy to hold. Then to the girl she handed a baton of bread and to her husband an object in a white cloth which when unwrapped revealed itself as a cold roast duck. Handling the corpse tenderly and cutting the strings that bound the limbs to the body, Monsieur explained to me that the duck was really an unfortunate that had been killed in an accident. It had been given to him by the owner as a gift of farewell, he said, as he divided it skilfully into four portions with his pocket-knife.

Watching other people eat is rarely a pleasant occupation, especially when their methods differ from one's own. I found it pleasanter to look out of the window and glimpse the live ducks in the passing farms. And while doing so I thought of a bird that once belonged to a Mr Regan in County Mayo. Regan was a man of little capital but great enterprise, and one day at a poultry show he bought with his last few shillings a prize drake—his 'stallion duck,' he called it. Asking a small fee for its services, he reaped such dividends that friends advised him to insure the creature. And then, a week after he had paid his first premium, a car met the drake neck on in a narrow lane. Regan carried the corpse to the insurance office and with tears in his eyes laid it on the agent's table. The agent, equally moved, said that he would take it home so that his wife could give it decent burial. Within a week Regan received a cheque for four times what he had paid for the bird. If he had not spent the money in celebrating its arrival, he might have launched out into even greater enterprise with pedigree stock.

As shortly after midday we approached Angers, the excitement grew. The children strained their necks at the window for the first sight of towers or spires. Madame having put on her shoes wrestled with the baggage from the racks. Meanwhile Monsieur wrote his new address on two pieces of paper and, with warm invitations to visit him if ever either of us stopped in Angers, gave one to my neighbour and the other to myself.

'Vous avez le vent en poupe' (meaning you have the wind behind you—you are lucky), said the sad-faced little man as he thanked him.

Angers 12.31, Nantes 13.46; change for La Rochelle, arrive 16.52.

At La Rochelle a bus took me to a ferry, the ferry took me to the harbour of Sablanceaux on the Île de Ré, and a taxi took me thence to the fishing village of La Flotte, some seven kilometres to the north-west.

CHAPTER TWO

Painting was now the order of the day. I was free to think in terms of colour rather than in those of black and white. There was no need to make the somewhat precise drawings from which I had been in the habit of designing my engravings, I could work direct, and the more calligraphic that work became the better—the pianist who has to search for his notes cannot achieve fluency, the work of a painter whose thoughts between brain and brush tip are interrupted by questions of technique must lack fire.

There was a time when I thought that nothing could be lovelier to draw or paint than the feminine variety of the human form, but I hadn't been long on the Île de Ré before I was convinced that the bows and sterns of fishing-boats offer quite as rich curves and a much greater variety of colour than anything to be seen on the throne of a studio.

In the harbour of La Flotte, a rectangular basin scarcely one hundred and fifty yards in length and less than half that in width, there is a daily pulse of movement—each tide a setting out or a return. While the water is low, boats lie on their sides dozing in their aromatic beds of mud, their nets like giant bat wings spread from mast to mast. But as the ocean seeps inward, following old channels in the slob and turning the groisy sludge to mirroring pools, men climb down the quay-bound iron ladders and make their way on board their vessels. No sooner are keels afloat than engines are started. Sun-tanned arms haul on vat-tanned sails. It may be several days before they return. Then, too, at flooding tide boats come home, the *Fleur do de Misère*, *La Blonde*, or the *Tralala*: shining cerulean, white or emerald, they moor against a quay backed by golden sunlit walls.

The colours of the fishing-boats are heraldic in their contrasts, and the ordering of those colours seems as traditional as the blazoning on a shield. Counter-change appears too. Where the hull strakes are blue above white or red above blue, the spars are white above blue or blue above red. Even the jackets and trousers of the men on board are strongly patterned with pale patches on dark, less faded cloth.

One evening as I sat at a café on the quay finishing a

small painting of some boats in the harbour, a young fisherman came to my table. He ordered a glass of red wine for himself and watched while I added a few last accents to the canvas. Then, leaning towards me and putting his hand on my arm, he asked very gently if I would paint a portrait of *his* boat? It was not so big as the one in my picture, he said, and some of its colour was faded, but he could tell me exactly how it ought to be. There followed a minute description of the colour scheme from mast to tip to water-line. He had a photograph, he said, which would help me with the drawing—he could leave it for me with the *patron* of the café. Then a worried look came into his face. How much would I charge? he asked.

It was an awkward question. 'I will do it for you as a gift,' I said.

His eyes lit up. 'And I will give you an aperitif,' he said with delight. Then he told me that the picture must be of his boat at sea, not in the harbour. He was giving me details of the sails that she carried when round the corner came a girl on a bicycle, her skirts bellying like a mainsail before the wind. 'Ma fiancée!' he exclaimed, leaping from his chair. He dropped fifteen francs on the table, the price of his wine, and was up and after her in less time than it would have taken me to change the brushes in my hand. I did not see him again and I never received the photograph. But I chanced one day to see his empty boat lying at low tide in the mud. She had no more colour on her than you'd find on a barnacle.

The production of salt and the culture of oysters are the

two chief industries on the island of Ré to-day, the former going back to Roman times, the latter of comparatively recent origin. About a century ago a Portuguese ship laden with oysters was wrecked off the coast, and the molluscs, dropping through the pierced bottom of the vessel, found conditions so much to their liking that they multiplied beyond belief. To-day, looking seaward from almost anywhere along the coast, one sees line upon line of heavily encrusted stones, acres of them in ordered ranks. One sees, too, men and women bent double with miniature pickaxes in hand, turning over the stones, selecting and separating the shells. Hard work, on their stoop, all through the hours of low tide.

Such is the importance of the industry that 'gamekeepers' have to be employed to keep away poachers who, alighting a moment from their cars, would carry away basketfuls of the shells. I gathered from one of these keepers that it is quite a simple thing to own an oyster *parc*. 'You just go along to the Syndicat Ostreicole and rent a strip of foreshore. Then you put down lines of stones, about the size of your head or a little larger, and you leave them there. No spawn is needed, there is plenty in the water, and at the end of three years you can collect oysters big enough to eat. Of course,' he went on, 'it is a good thing to clear them before eating by putting them for a few days in a reservoir free of mud, and if you want top grade for the Paris market you must select the best shells and spread them in a lagoon where there is a higher degree of nourishment for each shell—then in a few months they will be really fat.'

The salt marshes cover a wide area at the western end of the island. Shallow 'pans,' perhaps a thousand yards in length and divided into innumerable small rectangles by narrow clay footpaths, reflect the dazzling light. At sunset and dawn they resemble giant stained-glass windows, the intersecting lines of grey mud like the leads

dividing the units of glass. They have colours of their own, too, for there are salt-loving bacteria that tint the waters crimson and blue, and there are bright mosses and algae that thrive in the strong brine. Stripes of ripening wheat and barley between the pools add gold to the landscape, and small haycocks repeat in softer lines the pyramids of salt that, shining in the light, are like the ordered tents of miniature armies.

The depth of the water in the pans, at most a few inches, is carefully regulated by a sluice-gate hardly bigger than a playing card, and the salinity after long exposure in reservoirs is already high. It is not long before the crystals begin to form; it is not long before barefooted men are raking the salt into shining cones along the paths. Until a few years ago donkeys in their bright trousers transported it to the quayside; nowadays drab motors do the same work, braying their way among the marshes.

'This is the most beautiful part of the island,' said Monsieur René Renaud, an artist who lives at its western extremity, 'and yet there is nothing to paint, nothing but light. There are no subjects from which you can make a composition: there are no forms in the landscape, there is only light. And you must work quickly,' he said 'for it changes quickly. You see an effect and before you have set up your easel it has changed. If you have ten minutes to make the record you are more than fortunate.'

Monsieur Renaud, a middle-aged man of heroic proportions, had greeted me warmly when we met on one of the narrow roads that cross the marshes. 'You must pay me a visit,' he said.

A few days later I did so.

'It gives me my freedom,' he said, pointing to a kiln in the centre of his studio. 'Tourists do not buy large pictures, they buy small souvenirs. I paint the plates, the cups, the pots, and I fire them in the kiln, and I sell thousands. Then I am free to paint pictures.'

As becoming to an island noted for its *fruits de mer*, the majority of his subjects were marine. Anything from seaweed to sea-horses, from hermit-crabs to cuttle-fish, found their places in the gayest of colours on his plates, dishes, and ash-trays. He had, of course, the 'donkey in trousers' in profusion, but I noticed also an oft-recurring lady on a seashore pulling her shirt over her head. 'My grandfather,' said Monsieur Renaud, as I looked at one of these designs, 'was the keeper of the lighthouse at the end of the beach, *le Phare des Baleines* it is called—in the time of Tiberius three hundred whales were washed ashore there—and his wife was a *sage-femme* and all the ladies would go to consult her when—ah, here is my daughter,' he said, breaking off his discourse and introducing me to a girl of about sixteen. 'And that was how the beach got its name of *Trousse Chemise*,' he added. 'I think of the subject as *mon héritage*. I sell very many of it.'

On the wall of the studio was an oil-painting of a drowned fisherman lying on a beach, and I remarked on some lithographs of mermaids that hung alongside.

'Legends of Ré,' explained Monsieur Renaud. 'There are many of them.'

'All nonsense,' said Madame Renaud, who had followed her daughter and brought a tray with glasses and a bottle of home-made liqueur.

'I'm sure the siren one is true,' said the daughter.

'At one time there were sirens in the bay,' said her father. 'They lived on the rocks beyond the lighthouse and always they were attracting the fishermen from their wives. So one day a girl who had lost her fiancé in this way called all the women whose men had been enticed and they made a plan. That evening they went to confession and the next morning they received the sacrament. Then they went to the beach and took off their clothes and swam out into the sea. Each one had a small bottle of holy water tied in her hair. When they reached the rocks the sea was rough, but they could see the sirens in the foam.'

'They had big cold eyes like fish,' said the daughter.

'And don't forget the tails!' said her mother.

'When they saw the sirens,' continued Monsieur Renaud, 'they gave a great shout: "Give us back our men," and they threw their bottles against the rocks so that they broke and the holy water splashed on to the sirens, and no sooner had they done that than the sirens gave a terrible scream and dived into the sea and no one has seen them since.'

'And did the men come back?' I asked.

'Their bodies were cast up on the beach that night. That is one of them,' said Monsieur Renaud, pointing to his picture on the wall.

The girl turned to me. 'Have you sirens in your coun try?' she asked.

'Lots of them,' I said, 'but not with scales and tails: they wear fur like seals, and sometimes when they come ashore at night they take off the fur covering and they are just like other women. If a man can steal the fur, the girl must marry him.'

'Do your people believe *that?*' asked the mother.

'They believe anything in Ireland,' I said. 'They believe the devil himself often comes along in the shape of a black cat.'

'The devil once came to a fisherman here when he was hauling his net,' said Monsieur Renaud. ' "Count your fish," he said to the man. The fisherman counted. He had caught ninety-five. "That will be the number of your years," said the devil. The man died last year. His age was ninety-five.'

'But before he died,' ejaculated the daughter, 'he consigned to the devil all those who didn't believe his story!'

CHAPTER THREE

A T LE MARTRAY, on the isthmus that connects the two larger areas of Ré, there is less than a hundred yards between the sea on the south and the shallow lagoons on the north. On the ocean side sand stretches for miles to east and west, and behind the beach great dunes pile themselves in ever-changing forms. I had forsaken the rigid lines of the towns, thinking to find more varied patterns in the crinkled folds of those dunes; but I had forgotten wind, the begetter of such configurations. Day after day and all day during my two weeks at Le Martray the wind blew, and sand in tall plumes swept from the western horizon. It filled my shoes, it filled my pockets, it filled my ears; I felt that the hair on my head was becoming embedded in it like the marram grass that crested the dunes. Painting was impossible. I could only contemplate the successive wisps that whistled past and wonder at the regularity of the corrugations they created and the smoothness of the slopes they left behind, each grain as if dropped by chance yet each obeying a dozen laws of physics.

Looking south on a clear day I could see the Île d'Oleron, a stronghold of the Huguenots during the wars of religion. For sixty years they were in the majority and held sway on the island; but when in 1628 La Rochelle fell into the hands of Louis XIII, they were almost completely wiped out. Fifty-seven years later, on the revocation of the Edict of Nantes, many of the surviving families made their way into England and Holland. To-day, at most a few hundred Protestants remain on the island.

With the help of binoculars and perhaps a little imagination, I could also see the Île d'Aix, between Oleron and the mainland. It was from there that on 14th July 1815 Napoleon wrote his famous letter, casting himself on the mercy of the Prince Regent.

'Je viens, comme Thémistocle, m'asseoir au foyer du peuple britannique. Je me mets sous la protection de ses lois, que je réclame de Votre Altesse Royale, comme du plus puissant, du plus constant et du plus généreux de mes ennemis.' (I come, like Themistocle, to settle among the British people. I place myself under the protection of its laws, which I claim of Your Royal Highness as the most powerful, the most constant, and the most generous of my enemies.)

The fugitive Napoleon had come to the Île d'Aix three days earlier. Once a master of decisive action, now he could only vacillate. Various plans of escape were put before him, but he was unable to make a decision. Then, on 14th July, the Government of Louis XVIII decided that he was to be surrendered to the English. When Napoleon heard of this he put on full military uniform, and in the quiet of the night made his way to the harbour. From there a ship's boat took him to the French brig *L'Épervier* (the Hawk). Arriving on board he ordered the general who had accompanied him to return to shore:

'It must not be said that France handed me over to the English,' he told him. Next morning he was taken alongside the *Bellérophon*. As the emperor left the *Épervier*, he took water in the palm of his hand and three times sprinkled the hull of the ship that to him represented French soil. Then he sat down on a thwart and wept.

Liberté, egalité, fraternité: the first is the desire of every man on Ré, the second and the third are every day practice on the island.

An old man, lean and bearded, who stood beside a barrow loaded with sailors' peaked caps and berets, told me that he was 'un marchand ambulant de casquettes et chapeaux' and that he preferred his hand-barrow to a motor-van: it was less snobbish, he said. From the bottom of a beret-filled cardboard box he produced a photograph of his father, the founder of the business, and with it the first invoice to the firm, dated October 1876. The old man spoke with what he called 'un accent méridional,' and as he had only one tooth his words were difficult to follow. But I gathered that though he made the barest living from his *chapellerie*, he would rather push a barrow and be free than sit in a shop and be a slave. 'If you walk much you sleep well,' he said. He lived in the village of Ars, and when I spoke of the friendliness that I found everywhere on Ré, he said: 'There is a camaraderie on islands which you do not get on continents. It is because of the constant strife against the sea. The fields of the ocean are richer than those of the land, but the

gathering of the harvest is more dangerous. There is shelter from a storm on land, there is none at sea.'

Another inhabitant of Ré who had achieved his freedom was Paul Lemaitre, a strongly built man of middle age, sun-bronzed, and wearing when I met him a fisherman's blue jersey. He stopped me on the quay as I was passing a striped awning that had been erected beside a motor-van.

'You are a painter, Monsieur,' he said. 'I also am an artist. When I was young I worked at the Beaux Arts in Paris, I took prizes, I took a diploma. But when I left that school I could not sell my pictures. All that people asked of me was designs for their advertisements. That is not art, that is slavery.'

'And now?' I asked.

'Regardez mon atelier!' he said, pointing to the awning under which was arranged an assortment of buckets, basins, mugs, tubs, saucepans, watering-cans, and other utensils. 'On three days of each week I sell these in the villages; on four days of each week I am free to paint.'

Like most other refinements of civilization, this freedom

from introductions can have its disadvantages. One evening as I sheltered in the lee of the lighthouse, thinking lovely thoughts about the mud, a man sat himself down beside me and spoke in English. He had heard that I was a writer; he also was a writer, a translator. He had been an interpreter with a Scottish regiment during the war, and had learned their dialect; and as he had always been interested in marine engines, he had chosen Kipling's *Hymn of McAndrew* for translation. He then took many sheets of paper from his pocket and produced for me, in French with a Seaforth patois, the most painful phonetics that I have ever heard.

June 2nd—cold, wet, and windy. I was still at Le Martray, staying in the small hotel built with his own hands by Signor Enrico Silvestrini Borobo, an Italian mosaic mason who had remained in France after the war. 'Push the broken bits of glass, tiles, or pottery into the liquid cement and rub down with sawdust—plenty of sawdust, that's the secret,' he told me. On this particular day the household was in commotion because there had been an accident on the roads in the early hours of the morning, and Enrico had been called from his bed to take the shaken passengers to their homes. Not only that but the evening before he had painted all the window-frames on the front of his house, and during the night a sandstorm had ruined the work. Madame, his French wife, was *distraite* because that same morning she had found twenty of her week-old chicks almost dead from cold. Never had she known such wind and rain at that time of year. She had brought the chicks indoors and put them to sit on warm bricks, and at intervals she was pouring red wine down their throats; but she doubted if many would survive.

It was about midday when Enrico, to calm his nerves, began to tinker with his radio set. He had never had time to adjust it, he told me, but he hoped soon to have it in working order. He missed very much the opera from Milan.

From where I sat in the shelter of his trellised *patio* I could hear all the noises that a radio set in torment can emit. Then suddenly there was a pause and clearly over the air came in English the last words of a prayer: '. . . through Jesus Christ our Lord.' Another pause, and then in French, slowly and distinctly, the voice of a commentator: 'Il prend la couronne.' Another pause and then: 'Elle est couronnée.'

The commentary ceased—Enrico was still making adjustments. In spite of the detonations that followed I could see in my mind's eye the very act of the Archbishop, the reverence with which he took the crown and placed it on his sovereign's head, the gentle submission of the Queen, the quiet dignity of her peers in their sumptuous robes. Rarely, I thought, could so few words have conjured up so grand a scene.

Then Enrico came from indoors. 'That was England,' he said.

CHAPTER FOUR

THE END of June, but not the end of wind and rain; and in spite of such weather visitors from the mainland—'the continent,' the islanders called it—arriving in droves of lorries; and terraces of bathing-huts being erected on the sand-swept beach. I began to think that there might be more privacy in Paris; there would certainly be more shelter. Then by chance I was offered a lift in a private car to that city, and I accepted. Perhaps being end of term at the art schools I might hear of a studio for the summer months when most artists go to the country. So I thought.

But I was wrong. There seemed as little hope as ever. 'Get a large room in a small hotel,' I was advised. But small hotels rarely have large rooms and, if they do, two visitors in a bed are better than one artist at an easel, especially during the tourist season. Eventually I settled

in a small hotel in a narrow street off the Boulevard Montparnasse. There was no possibility of setting up an easel:
what with the bed, the basin, the *bidet,* and the baggage,
there was scarcely a trickle of space left for me to move
between one and the other. Never mind, I could draw.
That took up little extra space at home or abroad. During
the following weeks I drew everything I came across,
from centaurs trying to get out of the Tuileries Gardens
with squealing women on their backs, to policemen con-
trolling the traffic.

For these drawings I used a special drawing-board
which I designed many years ago and which has ever since
been invaluable. It consists of a piece of soft light wood
measuring some ten by eight inches, with hinged to it by
a strip of leather a piece of three-ply as cover. Inside on
the corners are fastened spring clips to hold six or eight
sheets of drawing-paper in position. By this means the
sheets can be interchanged easily, and when an opportune
moment occurs those that have been worked on can be put
into safe keeping. Thus the rubbing that so often occurs
in sketch-books is avoided, and should the owner per-
chance get a drenching nothing is lost but the day's work.
On the inside of all my jackets I have a pocket large
enough to hold the board and so I can wander as I will
with both hands free. It is a contrivance that anyone can
make at home and seems to me in every way superior to a
sketch-book.

In mid July there came a call to London. Illustrations

were wanted for a book—the gravers had their grip on me again. But my last night in Paris was a cheerful one. It was 14th July, the national holiday, and everywhere people were celebrating. Flags and coloured lights at every café, and chains of red and blue lamps strung through the trees on either side of the boulevards of Montparnasse. Dance bands had installed themselves on the pavements and everyone was dancing—wives with their husbands, fathers with children in their arms or astride their shoulders, lovers in close embrace. Family parties had settled round the tables of their favourite café, prepared to stay till dawn. Noisy youngsters in paper caps rushed to and fro, laughing and singing. A party of Breton peasants danced their native dances to the music of a small hand-organ and a guitar, the men wearing the traditional short jackets with embroidered collars, black trousers, and wide-brimmed black hats with streamers, the women with crisp white lace headdresses and full skirts of heavy material that billowed around them as they danced.

The evening before had also been eventful. Duty and a touch of love had taken me to the Gare de Lyon to greet a Canadian girl, Jeannette, who was passing through Paris on her way to Milan. We had only met once before, a few months earlier in London, but because she herself was an engraver and knew my work she had sent me food parcels during the war. Now I hoped to return the compliment with a food parcel for her journey, a box of chocolate truffles.

Platform 13, I was told, and there on either side of it I found a huge segmented snake of a train with carriages labelled Lausanne, Milano, Venezia, Beograd, Istanbul. The two trains stretched their length into the darkness, their forward carriages out of sight. Soon they would be hissing their way to the other side of Europe.

I walked the length of the platform searching for Jeannette. Through the carriage windows I could see passengers in the third class preparing to sit up for the night with no more than a hired pillow for comfort. Across one of the compartments from rack to rack, a young father was slinging a hammock for his infant, while fellow passengers watched good-humouredly. In the first and second classes travellers were contemplating the narrow beds on which they hoped to sleep away a part of their journey. A chef, pale as a powdered clown, leaned from the door of a restaurant car.

Around me on the platform rose a babel of voices; it seemed that the only people who spoke French were the porters. A harassed courier was calling the roll of his party of tourists, who fluttered round him like nervous pigeons. A group of musicians were clutching instrument cases of curious shapes. They scattered at the approach of a chain of trucks, on which from a high rail were suspended bicycles of every colour. A trolley pushed by a sad-faced woman held close-packed rows of books and gaudy magazines; another with a white-coated attendant offered pillows and blankets for hire.

But hunt as I would, I could see no sign of Jeannette.

Among all the fervent and repeated good-byes there was no one for me to kiss when officials began to call 'En voiture—fermez les portes, s'il vous plaît.' Suddenly and silently one of the trains began to move—towards Venezia, Milano, Beograd, Istanbul, and very soon afterwards the other followed.

The names of those cities were in my brain as a taxi took me back to Montparnasse. 'Venezia, Venezia, Venezia,' stuttered the motor. 'Beograd!' shouted the driver as we escaped a collision. 'Istanbul!' retorted the offender. And thoughts of Venice were still in my brain when I reached London two days later.

CHAPTER FIVE

CHIPS, CHIPS, crisp curling chips. For the next two months there was little sound in my studio in London save the purring of a graver through boxwood. But constantly I would hear echoing in my skull the words 'En voiture! En voiture!' and in my mind's eye I would see the bright lights of the Gare de Lyon and those two long black serpents waiting to issue into the darkness and make their way across Europe from capital to capital, even unto Istanbul beside the Golden Horn. And I would think of Venice, that city of sky and water, where reflections turn all reality into romance.

There came an afternoon when I had the honour of opening an exhibition of Bewick's engravings at the Bethnal Green Museum. His preliminary drawings, his blocks, his proofs and finished books, including the famous *Quadrupeds*, the *Birds*, and the *Fables*, had been collected from many sources and displayed superbly. The exhibition was to celebrate the bicentenary of the birth of the artist so often and so rightly called 'the father of modern wood-engraving.'

That same evening I met a patron of the Arts, one given to the collecting of illustrated books.

'Doing anything special these days?' he asked jovially.

'I've just been opening a magnificent exhibition of Bewicks,' I told him.

He paused a moment as if surprised. 'Yes,' he said thoughtfully, 'they are excellent cars.'

That was enough to blow anyone across the Channel. Two nights later I found myself again at the Gare de Lyon in Paris and this time it was I who from behind the curtains of a *couchette* watched the pale-faced people on the platform. Just as before, there were truckloads of bicycles serpentining through the crowds, trolleys with racks of mineral waters and pyramids of cigarettes halting before windows, women clutching hatboxes and handbags, coats and parcels, as they trotted in the wake of laden porters; much embracing, endless good-byes. Again the train moved out silently and without signal.

It was the only silent part of the journey. My compartment was near the engine, and as the night wore on

I wondered why it was called a sleeper. There were times too when I wondered if we were on or off the rails. I awoke finally to a morning grey with mist. All I could see from my window was field after field of sweet corn, the leaves withering, the fruit yellowing. At intervals we passed a village or a town where there would be a campanile and houses with low-pitched tiled roofs; then again more and yet more fields of corn.

I went into the restaurant car for coffee, to find a gentleman from overseas drinking double brandies. He was already 'noticeable', repeating many times to the attendants that he was going round the world in four and a half days' flying hours and that he was spending the afternoon in Venice. By ten o'clock he had 'drink taken', by eleven he was 'drunk'. When at midday we reached Venice, he was 'paralytic'. Later I heard that he made his way to the Piazza San Marco and there, falling on his face, scattered the pigeons and cut his skull. He had been taken to hospital and in due course put on the night train for Milan and thence to Karachi, Khartoum, or wherever next his travel vouchers were to carry him.

Meanwhile, quiet as a water bird, my gondola moved through the shine and glitter of the Grand Canal. I had no consciousness of motive power: perched astern, with feet splayed like a ballet dancer's, the gondolier plied his single oar, gently, soundlessly, with infinite ingenuity. On either side of the canal dream palaces competed with each other in the exuberant fancy of their façades: marble-pillared arches, round and pointed, rose from the water to support fretworks of other arches, pointed and cusped, and they in their turn bore arcades of yet finer and more intricate traceries. Windows, square, oval and round, framed in carved filigrees, filled the intervening spaces. Even the corners of the buildings had their braided or cabled ornament from water's edge to roof.

The high beak of the gondola swung into a narrow side canal whose waters were inky green. Colours became deeper, more intense: palaces gave way to tenements whose plastered walls were peeling, to warehouses whose massive wooden doors stood deep in water. We passed under one small rounded bridge after another, each of them connecting alleyways that later I was to know as major streets. House walls were of every colour—plum, apple-green, saffron or carmine, sun-worn tints mellow as ripened fruits; shutters too, ivory, cerulean, rose pink, sienna. Often our way was impeded by brightly painted craft loaded with vegetables and fruit, jars of wine, crates of glass ware; we passed a wherry low in the water with coal and timber, another with furniture of a household on the move. At every corner a call of warning, as elsewhere one hears a motor-horn. Then the shadowed walls opened to a blaze of light and again we were in the Grand Canal, the gondola rising and dipping to the swell of passing motor-boats. But only for a moment. We crossed the wide shimmering stretch and threaded our way through further tortuous channels, short cuts to that main reach of water where stood my hotel.

Venice is a city outside of time, decayed but not

decadent. It is a stage on which ghosts of the past are more substantial than the actors who to-day strut its boards. Present-day inhabitants have no reality: they move through the streets or across the Piazza like painted figures through whose thin pigment one may sometimes glimpse the background. They occupy the city as attendants occupy a theatre, impersonally, without other interest than to serve those who make up the audience and who may never pay a second visit to their show.

There are neither motor-cars nor bicycles in the city, the only traffic congestion is of pigeons. Neither is there dust: every street and square is paved. The widest streets are hardly more than alleyways: in the narrow ones two men carrying loads on their shoulders, or elsewhere, cannot pass. I often had to step aside to let a stout man go by. Clothes-lines strung across a street from window to window can barely hold two shirts abreast. And yet at night one wanders happily through a labyrinth of these dark passages, any of which in another city would be shunned in daylight. Everywhere there are subjects for drawing or painting, but to set up an easel would block the street, even to stand still awhile dislocates the ant-like processions. Everywhere too there are smells, in particular by some of the smaller canals at low tide. Perhaps to an inhabitant they have their charm—none of the human senses has greater variation of appreciation than that of smell. It is told of a man whose daily work was in a city sewer that one day, entering a flower shop, he was overcome by the perfumes and fainted. They carried him out into the fresh air without avail; it was only the effluvia of a passing refuse cart that brought him back to consciousness.

Compared with Paris, there are few artists to be seen in Venice, but one morning I found myself beside an extremely tall and thin man who was standing before a canvas almost as tall and thin as himself. He was trying to fit a colonnade of wide arches on to this narrow space. I couldn't help a remark to him in French that his canvas was an awkward shape for the subject. 'But no,' he said, 'I like my canvases of that proportion. I cannot paint on any other.'

'And when I paint,' I said, 'I like my canvases nearly square.'

A smile spread over his face as he pointed to our reflections in a shop window. 'It is not *par hazard*,' he said, 'that our tastes are different.'

I left him to his problem then, but after lunch we met again at a café overlooking the Grand Canal, when he introduced himself as Marcel Delort. He said that he had been much amused by our conversation of the morning, and went on to tell me that just before leaving Paris he had found a most superb model: so thin was she that the outlines of her limbs were straight, almost parallel, and scarcely separated. It was glorious to follow those twin lines with a pen. 'Perhaps you would not like them?' he suggested.

I pointed to a wherry that was making its way along

the canal. 'Bluff in the bows and rounded in the stern is more to my taste,' I said.

'C'est pas par hazard,' he answered again.

Our talk reverted to canvases and their proportions. I told him that I much preferred the standard French measurements to those in England, that I found the broader shapes more inviting, more stimulating. He said that in all rectangles that were aesthetically pleasing the measurements had a definite and significant mathematical relationship. Had I not heard of Pythagoras and the Golden Number?

All I knew of Pythagoras, I said, was his theorem about the square on the hypotenuse of a right-angled triangle being equal——

Delort interrupted me. 'Pythagoras believed,' he said, 'that the whole universe is governed by mathematical laws, even to the intervals between the stars. All harmonies in music, just as all harmonies in art, obey these rules.' While speaking he had drawn a rectangle on the marble-topped table between us. 'If we call that short side 1,' he said, 'and the long side 1.618, we have the Golden Rectangle. If now we draw a line to cut off a square on the 1, we have a rectangle of 0.618 × 1 at the other end, and those two sides are in exactly the same ratio to each other as the 1 is to the 1.618. And you can then make a square on the 0.618 and that will leave another rectangle with the same proportion, and so on until it becomes too small to draw.

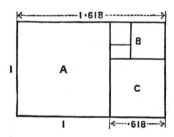

'Here is another piece of interest,' he continued as he drew a pentagon on the table and added diagonal lines from point to point. 'In the figure of five sides there is also the Golden Number. If each of those sides is 1, then each of the lines from point to point is 1.618.'

He got up and left me, for he had another mathematical problem in paint awaiting him near the Campo San Provolo.

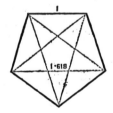

CHAPTER SIX

MACAULAY wrote of St Mark's Cathedral: 'I do not think it, nobody can think it, beautiful, and yet I never was more entertained by any building.'

Beauty, according to the *Oxford Dictionary*, is 'that quality or combination of qualities which affords keen pleasure to the senses, especially that of sight, or which charms the intellectual or moral faculties.' There is no doubt that this exuberant haphazard agglomeration of semi-precious stones does give pleasure to the senses, and charm the intellectual faculty of the normal human being whatever it may do to the moral disposition of the pendant. It is a heaped-up mass of happy accidents, with ornaments as illogical as tumbling clowns in a circus, always the unexpected at unexpected moments.

37

At the time of the building of this church in the eleventh century and for many years after, there was nothing that the Venetians would not do to embellish their city and, in such a frame of mind, it was but natural that in matters of decoration they should give precedence to the basilica that held the body of their patron St Mark. Of the many miracles and legends concerning the finding and preservation of that body, and of the many other sacred relics enshrined within the cathedral, I will leave to e of greater faith to speak. Time wedded to imagina-
' gets many prodigies.

B e fifteenth century Venice held complete supremacy at sea, and trading fleets of as many as five hundred vessels would leave her shores at regular intervals to gather the spices of the Moluccas, the pearls and sapphires of Ceylon, the broideries of Cashmere and other valuable commodities. For the adornment of their church marbles were brought from Greece, porphyries from Egypt, alabasters from Arabia: the masters of all ships trading in the eastern Mediterranean were instructed to collect precious stones wherewith to beautify the monument. Nor did those captains spurn the slave trade, often buying young girls in the ports of the Black Sea and bringing them back to be auctioned on the Piazza of San Marco. Though this trade was officially prohibited, it was carried on openly, and even within the religious orders transactions sometimes took place. Jacopo Filiasi, the eighteenth-century Venetian historian, quotes a contract which tells that in 1428 a Russian female slave was sold by one friar to another for fifty-two sequins, with 'right to dispose of her body and soul in perpetuity.'

Inside St Mark's there is a great calm. At one's feet patterns in the paved floor change and counter-change in infinite variety; overhead, mosaics sparkle on golden vaults. In contrast to the turmoil on the outside walls, all within is delicately ordered.

Ruskin likened the mosaics to the pages of a vast illuminated missal from which the people of the time learned their scripture history. Tale after tale from Old and New Testaments is unfolded in these pictures so clearly that the most unsophisticated can read their meaning, so cunningly that the most sophisticated will delight in their art. On the shimmering golden pages of this missal we find not only naïveté but gentle humour. Among the animals that await their turn to be loaded into the Ark is a large black bull with a ring in its nose; after the Flood one lion drops on to a peak of Ararat, as if thrown from the Ark, while Noah hauls the other by the scruff of its neck through a window. All the designs are superb and, in such a reluctant medium, the details are amazing. Differences between quail and partridge are as clearly shown as between peacocks and geese. The foliage in Eden is worthy of Paradise, and might have been painted by Rousseau *le douanier*. As in the panels of Adam and Eve, there is no prudery in those of the drunken Noah. Salome dancing in medieval dress with trailing fur-trimmed sleeves is none the less convincing. The Flight into Egypt and the Baptism of Christ might have been designed by Mantegna.

Opening from the narrow streets of the city are innumerable squares and courtyards, and in most of these may be seen marble well-heads, often richly carved. Until close on a century ago, when pipe-lines were laid

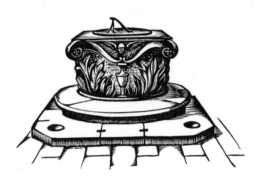

from the mainland, Venice depended almost entirely on these wells for her water supply, and she acknowledged their importance by giving them capitals that rank among the finest sculpture in the city. The simpler ones have no more than foliated corners with a device, symbolic or heraldic, on the sides; but others are ornate not only with richly carved pillars but with cherubs, peacocks, eagles and, as befitting to the city of St Mark, lions in profusion.

As there were no fresh-water springs in this sea-borne city, the functioning of the wells depended almost entirely on rain, and they were designed to meet this limitation. A deep pit as wide as space permitted was dug and, after a central shaft of porous brick had been built, was filled in with gravel and sand. The well-head was then set in place, and the surrounding area paved in such a way that rain falling on it could percolate through perforated stones into the sand and gravel beneath. Thence, filtered, it passed through the bricks and their interstices into the cavity of the well. In times of drought water was brought in barrels from the mainland and spilled on to the paving-stones. From there it would follow the same course as did the blessing from heaven and, however brackish it might have been on arrival, would reach the surface a second time clear and sparkling as from a spring. Cut in the steps that form the base of many of these well-heads are small circular cups to hold water. They are for the birds, I was told. A kindly thought, it seemed; and then I remembered that St Francis in his travels had spent a while in Venice. Were those pools an echo of his visit? I wondered.

CHAPTER SEVEN

IN MY BOOK *Sweet Thames Run Softly* I have told how on my first visit to Venice I was mistaken for St John by one who, striding down the Piazza in long robes, had all the semblance of Donatello's St Mark. This time it was my nationality rather than my saintliness that came into question. It happened one day as I lunched in my hotel that I heard in strident accents from across the room: 'I may not be very good mor-ally, but I certainly am great financially.' Others also had heard the remark, and a momentary hush fell upon the company. As I looked around to discover the source of such a statement, its author caught my eye.

'Say,' he barked, 'what part of the States do *you* come from?'

Heaven was with me. In my softest cadences I replied that I came from a small island off his eastern seaboard, not yet annexed.

The effect was splendid. Others of his nationality turned in their chairs and made gestures of approval. Three beautiful girls from Brazil smiled at me from a far corner. I wished that I could have dallied awhile. But the sun was shining, and there was a painting of a golden wall reflected deep into one of the narrow waterways which I had begun the afternoon before.

Leaving the hotel I made my way across the great Piazza, and thence by narrow streets towards the subject of my painting. On the bank of a canal I passed a post-man delivering letters. Rather than climb steep stairs, he rang the street door-bells and waited till baskets were let down from the appropriate windows. In a courtyard a group of men and women were following a coffin to a waiting gondola. At the water's edge a priest sprinkled holy water, giant wreaths of flowers were handed on board, and after the coffin had been draped in purple and black the floating hearse moved slowly away in the direction of the island cemetery. In its wake a shining mahogany motor-launch carried the priest and mourners.

As I pursued my course through the tortuous streets there seemed to be scarcely a door whose archway was not carved, and constantly I noticed on the walls images of saints, shields of arms, or grotesque heads in stone. It must have been looking at these that made me lose my way—easy enough at any time in Venice. When at last

I found the golden wall the sun had left it, and instead of a blaze of honey-coloured light all was in cool shadow.

My feet were weary from the wandering and I was glad when a gondolier offered me a lift. The tide was high and I think he was glad of a little weight in his craft, for as we passed under some of the lower bridges the metal prow scraped the apex of the arch and he had to crouch low on his after-deck. We passed through narrow waterways, silent and chill, where disembodied hands adjusted a shutter or shook a cloth out of a window above our heads. Gently, almost caressingly, we rounded a last corner and, emerging into sunlight, moored beside the Doge's Palace.

By now it was the hour of fashion on the Piazza and the café tables were filled with a concourse of many nationalities. Strolling in the square were officers of police in blue and scarlet tail-coated uniform, with tricorne hats and swords; stout nursemaids with white stockings and aprons pushed perambulators among the pigeons. There were Austrian boys in Tyrolean hats and Scots boys in kilts, and groups of local girls, small and plump, with long earrings and the highest of heels. There were brown-robed friars and black-robed priests, and a man with a broom and a scuttle-shaped box at the end of a long handle: but for the pigeons he would have been out of a job.

The mingled music of three orchestras encompassed me as I crossed the square. I was looking for a seat where I could hear but one repertoire at a time when I was hailed by Delort and invited to his table.

He introduced me to his companion, Marie, a French girl. I did not catch her surname.

'I thought that I would meet you,' said Delort, as we sat down. He took from his pocket a copy of *The Merchant of Venice*. 'You see,' he continued, as he took a marker from the pages, 'your English poet was a follower of Pythagoras.' He pointed to the lines where Gratiano, addressing Shylock, says:

> 'Thou almost mak'st me waver in my faith
> To hold opinion with Pythagoras,
> That souls of animals infuse themselves
> Into the trunks of men.'

'Did Pythagoras believe in transmigration then?' I asked.

'It was one of his special teachings,' said Delort.

I was afraid for a moment that I was in for another philosophical discussion, but the presence of Marie saved the situation. Petite and trim, with her fair hair in a coil around her head, she had a sketch-book open on the table before her.

'Monsieur was explaining to me about the gondolas,' she said.

'What's the matter with them?' I asked.

'They're difficult to draw,' she said.

'It is because the two sides are not the same,' said Delort. 'The side on the left of the middle line is wider than the one on the right. That makes a balance for the

45

one oar of the gondolier which is on the right. They are not easy to draw.'

I asked him if he knew why, with the people of Venice so fond of colour, all the gondolas should be black.

'It was a doge who made the command,' he said. 'It

was to stop the extravagance. No more crimson and gold on the gondolas!'

Delort was anxious for talk but I was anxious for drawing, so leaving him with his girl I went back to the hotel and exchanged paint-box for drawing-board. I was lucky that evening in that as it fell dark I came upon the Ponte San Provolo in strong light from a hidden lamp, and I was lucky too that only as I was putting a last touch to my drawing of it did a sudden shower drive me into shelter.

The rain that began that evening went on for days. It teemed unceasingly. Cascades were spewed from gutters overhead, water welled up between the paving-stones from underground. It was the time of high tides and a strong wind piled the waters even higher. Along the sea front waves rolled in over the Piazzetta to join the rising lakes ashore. Normally the surface of the Piazza appears flat, but as the floods rose different levels showed themselves: on the highest of these, trestle causeways, hurriedly constructed, offered the only means of transit from one side of the square to the other. Many of the streets became impassable except on the backs of porters who, in high rubber boots and oil-skins, did a thriving trade. Passengers coming ashore from the water-buses had likewise to be carried across the landing-stages. The ground floors of shops and houses were flooded, a foot deep or more.

'But we are accustomed to it,' said the manager of my hotel as I watched the staff rolling up the carpets and carrying the furniture to higher levels. 'We have a saying,' he said, 'for a man who has drunk too much, that he is suffering from *aqua alta*, the high water.'

'Half-seas over in English,' I said.

He nodded in agreement.

Delort had spoken of how the curbing of luxury in the fifteenth century had affected the colour of gondolas even to the present day. It was five centuries earlier that another restriction on extravagance gave birth to what is now an everyday word in the English language. At that earlier date it was the custom in Venice on St Mark's Day for all the affianced daughters of the nobility to repair to the church of San Pietro di Castello carrying with them their dowries, and there to meet their future husbands. Twelve poor girls of the city whose dowries had been given by the Doge would also go there for the same purpose, and all together they would hear Mass and the bishop would bless them. Then each bridegroom would take his bride and lead her to his home.

In the year 943 some pirates from Istria, thinking to make a profit by this custom, laid in wait on the appointed day, raided the church almost as the blessing was being pronounced, and carried away both brides and dowries. But the Doge, who was present, immediately assembled a force, and following the robbers came upon them in what is still known as the Porto delle Donzelle, the Port of the Damsels. Then, having rescued the maidens and their coffers, he returned to Venice, and in due course to commemorate the event he instituted the 'Feast of the Maries.' Each year on the appointed day twelve poor girls, richly dowered by the city, were led in solemn state to the church of Santa Maria Formosa, there to give thanks to the Blessed Virgin for her protection of their sisters. Pageants and regattas followed and, as the historian da Canale writes: 'If you had been there you would have seen the whole waters covered with boats filled with men and women, so that no one could count them, and a throng of dames and damsels at the windows and on the banks, apparelled so richly that none in Venice might surpass them.'

Eventually the festival became so sumptuous that the Council of the Republic had to step in and limit the extravagance, even to substituting wooden figures for the twelve Maries—puppets that became known as Marionetti; hence our word, marionette.

In 1295 Marco Polo, with his father and uncle, returned to Venice after twenty-four years' absence. They came ashore from their galley wearing the rough dress of Tartar peasants. Their faces were weather worn, their hair unkempt; they had forgotten much of their native speech. Small wonder that they received but scanty welcome from the distant relatives who by then were inhabiting the old home. There was not only incomprehension but suspicion on their part, for they had long believed the travellers to be dead. They suggested to the 'strangers' that they should continue with their voyaging. How those strangers persuaded them to the truth is as pretty a tale as anything that Marco had to relate. Perhaps in the course of centuries it did not lose in the telling, but the greater part of it is on the testimony of one Ramusio, a distinguished citizen of Venice during the fifteenth century, whose family for many generations had lived in the same parish as the Polo family and who had often heard the story from the descendants of the voyagers. From what he tells us we gather that the three Polos had not been unobservant of human nature while on their travels. Finding but a poor welcome at home, they prepared a great banquet and invited all the relatives. Then, when the guests were assembled, 'the three came out of their chamber dressed in long robes of crimson satin, according to the fashion of the time, which touched the ground. And when water had been offered for their hands, they placed their guests at table, and then taking off their satin robes put on rich damask of the same colour, ordering in the meanwhile that the first should be divided among the servants. Then after eating something (no doubt a first course), they rose from table and again changed their dress, putting on crimson velvet, and giving as before the damask robes to the servants, and at the end of the repast they did the same with the velvet, putting on garments of ordinary cloth such as their guests wore. The persons invited were struck dumb with astonishment at these proceedings. And when the servants had left the hall, Messer Marco, the youngest, rising from the table, went into his chamber and brought out the three coarse cloth surcoats in which they had come home. And immediately the three began with sharp knives to cut open the seams, and tear off the lining, upon which there poured forth a great quantity of precious stones, rubies, sapphires, carbuncles, diamonds, and emeralds, which had been sewed into each coat with great care, so that nobody could have suspected that anything was there. For on parting with the Great Khan they had changed all the wealth he bestowed upon them into precious stones, knowing certainly that if they had done otherwise they never could by so long and difficult a road have brought their property home in safety. The exhibition of such an extraordinary and infinite treasure of jewels and precious stones which covered the table, once more filled all present with such astonishment that they were dumb and almost beside themselves with surprise: and they at once recognized these honoured and venerated gentlemen of the Ca' Polo whom at first they had doubted, and received them with the greatest honour and reverence. And when the story spread abroad in Venice, the entire city, both nobles and people, rushed to the house to embrace them, and to make every demonstration of loving kindness and respect that could be imagined.'

On the site of the house where Marco Polo lived in Venice there is now a cinema. He died in 1324 and was buried in the church of San Lorenzo, but the tomb was later transferred to the courtyard and to-day its site is unknown. John Masefield has written: 'It is only the wonderful traveller who sees a wonder, and only five travellers in the world's history have seen wonders. The others have seen birds and beasts, rivers and wastes, the earth and the (local) fullness thereof. The five travellers are Herodotus, Gaspar, Melchior, Balthazar, and Marco Polo himself. The wonder of Marco Polo is this—that he created Asia for the European mind.'

CHAPTER EIGHT

I T IS A common experience with artists of other countries to find their creative faculties numbed when confronted with the aesthetic achievement of Italy. Venice in particular is unnerving in that everything that could be said about its palaces or its warehouses has already been said by the stones themselves. There is nothing to be added to or subtracted from their self-expression, individual or collective. Contrary to the rules of logic, art is a progression from the particular to the universal; but there is nothing of the universal to be found in the façades of Venice, the city is unique. When Turner painted there he painted light, not Venice. When Whistler etched there he etched not Venice but Whistler, the same Whistler that he found on the Thames. Only a Canaletto or a Guardi could paint *Venice,* and both of them have already done so. The city to-day is as they recorded it, with but the fourth dimension, time, added.

There were moments when I felt that the city might be of glass. The sky was reflected in the water and the water cast back its opal to the sky and, somewhere between the two, iridescent cupolas and spires rose from a stippled haze. It seemed but fitting then that for centuries the Venetians should have occupied themselves with the creation of fantasies in glass. In every sunlit street, in every shadowed alleyway, candelabra and vases, fishes, pheasants, and gim-

crack souvenirs sparkled and shimmered in the shops—
miracles of craftsmanship, with every possibility of the
material exploited to the utmost. There are people who,
mistaking artifice for art, admire these products; I found
the achieving of them more interesting than the achievement.

In the year 1292, to avoid the danger of fires, the glass-
works on the main island were transferred to Murano, one
of the smaller islands in the lagoon, and it was there that
I saw some of the work in progress. I watched a man take
from a furnace a long metal tube at whose far end glowed
a golden ball of molten glass. Rotating it quickly so that
the ball did not lose its shape, he handed it to his partner
who sat at a nearby anvil. This man, still rotating the
tube, blew gently into the mouthpiece; the glass swelled
into a bubble and then into a sphere; by some mysterious
sleight of hand the sphere became a bowl. A moment
later a pliant ribbon from the furnace, twisted a few times
to give it rope-like form, was added as a handle. The
bowl had become a basket.

At the next furnace incandescent pokerheads were being manipulated as if they were pastry, to become leaves
for epergnes. At another, in less than five minutes, a
molten globule became a shining horse. First on the anvil
the body was touched into shape with hammers, then with
pincers the legs and ears were drawn out, the curly mane
crimped, the tail contrived.

It was at Murano that, more than a century ago, the
glass paperweight as we know it to-day originated. Mr

E. M. Elville, in his delightful book *Paperweights and Other Glass Curiosities,* tells us how, by a process similar to that used for other purposes in Egypt during the fifteenth and fourteenth centuries B.C., the exquisite little florets are built up and combined within their crystal spheres. I had always been dumbfounded by these curios, wondering how, short of divine intervention, they could have been produced. Now I know that, each of the many florets is born of a multi-coloured cluster of glass rods fused together and while still molten drawn into a thread whose sections are as flowers. That is the secret of their creation.

My mother once owned a fine example of these *millefiore* weights—we kept it on the mantelpiece of the drawing-room at the Rectory. It had been given to her by her father, a great collector of everything elegant or historical. His only trouble in life that I, as a boy, knew of was that he always wanted to share the delight of his latest acquisition. If a daughter of his when visiting him admired it, his immediate reaction would be: 'Take it home with you, girl! Take it home!'

And then in the course of a few weeks or a few months he'd be visiting the girl's house, and he'd see maybe the same helmet-shaped silver cream jug, or the Waterford glass mustard pot, or perhaps the paperweight. 'Oh, that's a daisy—where did you find that?' he would say.

'Why, Father, you gave it to me.'

'Did I give you that? Did I give you that? Are you sure 'twas I gave it to you?' And his hands would finger it lovingly and he would put it down with such an air of regret that the only possible answer was: 'But, Father, wouldn't you like to have it back?' And he would say: 'Well, lend it to me just for a little while.'

And then perhaps a month later another daughter seeing it in his study would admire it, and the same cycle of events would take place.

Tintoretto's *Last Judgment,* that covers the whole of one wall in the Ducal Palace, is said to be the largest painting on canvas in the world. Many of the same artist's other paintings are enormous too; but size in art is no criterion. However stupendous in design and execution his *Marriage at Cana* and his *Presentation of the Virgin* in the church of Santa Maria dell-Orto, or his *St Mark rescuing a Slave* in the Accademia, may be (all three measure about twelve by twenty feet), they lack the vitality and intensity that we find in works on the same scale by Paolo Veronese. In the sixteenth century it was common for an artist's studio to be a family business, in which sons and daughters took part in the work and of which membership was jealously guarded. When a pupil of Tintoretto's made a proposal of marriage to his daughter Ottavia, he was told yes, if he should prove himself a painter worthy of the house.

To my way of thinking almost all of Tintoretto's work suggests a commercial approach. The grand groups of figures are but assortments and re-assortments of stock drawings. There is scarcely a figure that might not be an academic pose cleverly fitted in where occasion demanded. Pictures were 'turned out' from his workshop, and in almost all of them we can see the model holding the pose. Not so, however, with his four allegorical paintings of Venus, Bacchus, Ariadne, and other divinities which decorate one of the smaller rooms of the Ducal Palace. In the *Last Supper* in San Giorgio Maggiore we see figures from the throne of any art school; but when in the Ducal Palace the exquisite ethereal Venus floats across the sky to place a diadem on the head of Ariadne, who symbolizes Venus, we know that the painting was done not from a model but from Venus herself, who paused a moment while the artist worked.

Like that of Tintoretto, the workshop of Paolo Veronese was also a family affair, so much so that after the death of the artist the business was carried on by his sons, his brother, and his nephew under the style of 'Heirs of Paolo.' But Paolo did not play at jigsaws with studio properties. Each of his figures is entirely convincing as a personality: there is no hint of search for an appropriate pose.

Bernard Berenson, writing of this artist, gives us an interesting sidelight on the religious life of the period. 'It is curious,' he says, 'to note that Paolo's chief employers were the monasteries. His cheerfulness, and his frank and joyous worldliness, the qualities, in short, which we find in his huge pictures of feasts, seem to have been particularly welcome to those who were expected to make their meat and drink of the very opposite qualities. This is no small comment on the times, and shows how thorough had been the permeation of the spirit of the Renaissance when even the religious orders gave up their pretence to asceticism and piety.'

And as a pendant to this we have the words of Vasari, the contemporary artist and historian: 'Among other things my fancy led me to represent a lecherous Satyr, hidden in the bushes and gloating over the sight of the naked Venus and the Graces. This so delighted the cardinal that he got me to begin a new and larger picture of a combat of satyrs with fauns, nymphs and infants, practically a Bacchanal.'

In contrast let Vasari speak again, this time of Jacopo Bellini and his sons.

'Jacopo had two sons,' he writes, 'devoted to the arts and possessing great ability, the one Giovanni, the other Gentile, named after Gentile da Fabriano, his dear master, who had been like a loving father to him. When these boys were grown, Jacopo himself taught them the principles of design with all diligence. But it was not long before they both far surpassed him, to the delight of their father, who incited them to endeavour to out-strip each other, competing as the Tuscans did, so that Giovanni should beat him, then Gentile both of them, and so on. . . . Although the brothers lived apart, they bore such a respect for each other and for their father that each one declared himself to be inferior to the other, thus seeking modestly to exceed the other no less in goodness and courtesy than in the excellence of art.' Later Vasari says of

Giovanni that he had many pupils 'because he taught all with pleasure,' and that eventually when he had 'attained to the age of ninety years, he died of old age, leaving an immortal name by the works which he produced in his native Venice and elsewhere.'

It was Giovanni who painted that superb portrait of the Doge Leonardo Loredan that hangs in the National Gallery in London. It was his hand that limned the calm features of a man strong enough in character to withstand all the powers of Europe when by the League of Cambrai in 1508 they had joined forces against Venice.

There are many of Giovanni's paintings in Venice, almost all of them religious in their intention; but it is not so much the stylized figures that give delight as the glimpses of landscape that form the backgrounds. Winding roads lead to cities whose towers and turrets are lovely as those of Venice herself; behind the cities rise line upon line of mountain peaks, more splendid than the Alps in greatest glory.

CHAPTER NINE

ROM VENICE in the diocese of Gibraltar, with
the Archdeacon of Tanganyika as officiating
minister, I found myself again within sound
of the bells of St Cuthbert's in the diocese of
London. But I fear it was not upon the blessed Cuthbert
that my thoughts tended to dwell, nor upon the otters
which, after he had come ashore from praying neck deep
in ice-cold water, would dry his feet with their fur and
warm them with their breathing. Instead, it was the
genial island of Tahiti, and the arrival there in 1767 of the
first European ship, that occupied my mind. The reason

for this relapse in thought was that my friend Charles Ede of the Folio Society had directed me once more to my engraving table, saying that he needed some illustrations for a special edition of *The Discovery of Tahiti* by George Robertson, sailing master of H.M.S. *Dolphin*.

These decorations (one of which by gracious permission I now reproduce) presented me with no great difficulties, for I know the country around Matavai Bay, where the *Dolphin* had lain at anchor. I had indeed waded in the fresh-water stream from which the sailors of the ship had filled their breakers, and had often drunk the milk of coco-nuts from the same palm groves in which those men refreshed themselves.

Robertson has given us a neatly expressed narrative of events during the stay of the *Dolphin* in that harbour. After the inevitable mutual suspicions of the first few days had died down and emblems of peace had been exchanged, there followed an idyllic month on board and on shore before the ship sailed again. What Robertson describes as 'the old trade' flourished, with nails as currency, and apart from the carpenter when he found his store of that commodity had been rifled by the crew, there was no ill will on any side.

By chance I still had a drawing of the mouth of the Vaitepiha river on the far side of the island, a 'fine pleasant valley' that Robertson had observed from his ship. He speaks of seeing great numbers of houses and several very good plantations, but in the 160 years between his visit and mine the whole island had suffered sad changes;

regions that were then thickly populated and under cultivation had become desolate. On the day I made my drawing, the mouth of that river was a pleasant situation, for with a light breeze from the sea there were no mosquitoes. Only the day before, when I had sought the source of a neighbouring stream, I had been driven back by the hordes of these pests which in the bamboo groves and among the clumps of *mape* trees had descended upon me like cloudbursts.

The technical problems of an artist's trade at home become multiplied when he visits the tropics. Mr. Parkinson, who accompanied Captain Cook on his first voyage to Tahiti two years after the visit of the *Dolphin,* found that the flies 'among other mischief, made it almost impossible for him to work, for they not only covered his subject so as that no part of its surface could be seen but even eat the colour off the paper as fast as he could lay it on.'

Apart from such external irritants, paper and pigments (like tourists freed of their tribal taboos) sometimes behave in unorthodox ways. When I was in Samoa I began a pencil portrait, in profile, of an old lady of the island. It was only when I came to put some delicate tones on the angle of her jaw that I sensed a roughness under my pencil, a roughness that in spite of all my efforts produced a series of circular blotches on her skin, as if of ringworm. How, without the language, could I explain to one proud of her complexion that the hot moisture of the tropics had produced a fungus in my chalk-surfaced paper?

As I dug my little chips from the boxwood blocks I

could not help thinking of other ships that within a few years of the *Dolphin's* arrival had visited Tahiti and anchored in Matavai Bay. Captain Cook came there in the *Endeavour* in 1769 and in the *Resolution* in 1774 and 1777. In 1789 Captain Bligh, with botanists on board from Kew Gardens, seeking young breadfruit-trees for the West Indies, cast anchor from the *Bounty*. Writing in his journal of Matavai and its neighbouring district, Opare, he says: 'These two places are certainly the paradise of the world, and if happiness could result from situation and convenience here it is to be found in the highest perfection.' We know the sad aftermath of his stay.

Eight years later came the *Duff* bearing the first missionaries who, more appropriately than they knew, chose as the opening hymn of their first service, 'O'er the gloomy hills of darkness.' By this time ships of other nations had also cast anchor and clouds had begun to form over this 'paradise of the world.' Men and women were wondering at the strange rotting diseases that had afflicted them since the coming of an alien race.

The disintegration of ancient Tahiti was epitomized for me when one day with James Norman Hall, the American author, I made an excursion into the now almost uninhabited eastern end of the island. As the track petered out we saw watching us from behind a tree a girl, pale and ghost-like, clad only in a few rags. She seemed frightened when we waved a greeting to her, yet she beckoned as if inviting us to follow her. We did not do so and she came no closer.

'So that is where Mata is living,' said Hall. Then he told me that until a few years earlier she had been the beauty of the island. But misfortune had overtaken her, not only in one form but in another. It was even rumoured that she had leprosy as well. The authorities had taken her and put her in hospital, but she had escaped. Now in this lonely bush, existing only on wild fruits and roots, she would live out her years, a few at most. Had we had any semblance of officialdom we would not have seen her, but Hall was known to everyone on the island. She had no fear that he would disclose her hiding-place.

Hall settled in Tahiti shortly after the First World War and, in collaboration with his fellow countryman Charles Nordhoff, wrote three highly successful books concerning the mutiny on the *Bounty*. Slight of build and gentle in manner, he was strong in kindliness: 'Jeemee' to his Tahitian wife, 'Papa Halli' to the natives of the island, 'my best friend' to every man that I have met who had ever met him. He died in 1951 and was buried as he had wished on the steep hillside behind his house. From his grave one can look down on Matavai Bay where, nearly two hundred years ago, the islanders saw that first European ship, the *Dolphin,* and where a few years later, in Hall's own words, 'Captain Bligh brought his ship the *Bounty* to anchor in thirteen fathoms.'

CHAPTER TEN

WHILE STILL in London I had an invitation to a wine-tasting from the firm of Smith & Hoey in Cooper's Row, E.C. Down in the stock lift I went, like any old barrel, to find in the cellar below, stretching away into the dimness, a long linen-covered table on which stood bottles innumerable. They were arranged in groups and before each unit stood glasses. 'I will leave you,' said my host, most graciously.

This was the kind of thing that Abū Nuwās in *The Arabian Nights* had dreamed of. Here was I in London with the reality before me. Gradually the cellar filled with rosy-faced gentlemen. There was no announcing: quietly as tobacco smoke may filter across a room they came in, though God knows if as much as one cigarette had been lit there'd have been a massacre. These gentlemen bent over the table, scanning the pedigree of each wine, and then, raising their part-filled glasses, commented on the colour, the nose, the body, the past, and the future of the vintage.

I noticed that sheen on hair and silver lights on glasses were not unlike, that tints in glass and tints on cheeks had their affinities; and then, standing back a moment, I realized that something of the classic curves of arches could be repeated in the human form. I made a few notes, intending to do a painting on the morrow. It is strange how one's vision changes over-night—sometimes you'd think there had been a week between p.m. and a.m.

Next morning, standing before my easel, I found a dearth of detail in my sketches. I needed a model. All right—ring up an agency. I had been told of a Mrs Mackenzie—she would surely provide.

She did. In reply to my inquiry she sent me a typewritten list of about a hundred names of men and women, the latter slightly predominating in numbers. If I would glance at the details given and let her know any that might be suitable, she would give me further particulars.

The information was arranged in columns: name, age, height, colour of hair, and then a few personal notes which, as in *Who's Who,* were doubtless supplied by the personality him or herself. As the ladies were given precedence in the schedule, I glanced first at their attributes. There was No. 12, aged twenty-three—Spanish type. There was No. 16, at the age of forty-two taking 'action poses.' No. 17, aged twenty-one, had 'exquisite colouring.' Nos. 22 and 23 were Parsee twins, gipsy costume. No. 27 had a figure 'neat and compact.' No. 32 was 'gamin type.' No. 49 had 'very firm bust, good legs, for private artists only.'

But it was a male that I sought, one who could play the part of a well-to-do business man or a retired cavalry officer. I noticed in the list that whereas the women had given bust, waist, and hip measurement, the men added thigh, calf, weight, and sometimes chest expansion. No. 62, aged forty, was 'very muscular.' No. 64, aged twenty-eight, had a 'slim subtle figure.' No. 69 had 'boxing physique.' No. 73 at fifty-seven years of age was 'gentlemanly, of good appearance.' No need to look further—that seemed what I wanted. I rang up Mrs Mackenzie.

'Yes,' she answered, 'he's a little bit cranky but I think he's what you want. Dookery is his name, though they call him Duke.'

Mr Dookery arrived at my studio next day punctually, a stately figure in the conventional dark suit that I had requested. He told me that it was mere chance that he was free, so many artists needed him, all the portrait-painters. He didn't think much of landscape painting, that was only nature: portrait-painting was Art, real Art. Yes, he was prepared to make an exception and pose as a gentleman for me, but he was accustomed to higher rank. Generals and admirals were his regulars; mayors he did too, and principals of universities—chancellors they called them. But what he liked most and where he felt at home was when he was doing royalty or the peerage. 'Twas a question of the dress—the robes or the uniform. But as his wife often said to him: 'The face is a small matter, it's the figure below it that one looks at.'

I asked him if he had sat much for the nude figure.

'As a young man, yes. I am on many of the best monuments in London,' he said. 'Marble friezes of the Empire. Of course, they changed the face for the different countries—but then, as my wife says, it's the figure that matters.'

He had posed for Academy pictures, too—'the old-style

66

ones, highly polished, took 'em months to do. Poses weren't by the hour in those days. I did Mercury for a man by the name of Wilson—every day for two months, on one foot with arms wide. I did a six weeks' Endymion for a lady after that—bit of a change, just lying down and going to sleep. And I did Pan for a gentleman—he wasn't an artist, just a major. But he was hung all the same, on the line in the Academy under another name. Now that man had breeding—the way he would say to me of a morning: "Mr Dookery, will you join me in a glass of wine?" Never seen it since. 'Twas with him I first met my wife. She was the nymphs for Pan, had to wear a bit of drapery. I was wearing trousers, 'cause all that was wanted was the torso. "The legs are goat's legs," said Sir William—that was his name, "they represent the earthy side of our nature; the beauty of our human heads and torsos expresses the higher attributes. Pan means all, everything," he said. Well, so it does, doesn't it? You can tell that by the papers—pan this and pan that.'

Just then I heard noon striking from St Cuthbert's. 'Will you join me in a glass of sherry wine?' I asked.

Mr Dookery put down the empty glass which he had held while posing and bowed. 'Thank you, he said, accepting a full one. 'Yes,' he added, 'Sir William was a proper gentleman. My boy Willie is a corporal in the Coldstreams now, but he never lets on his godfather carried a crown on his shoulder strap.'

CHAPTER ELEVEN

THE EYE of winter had begun to wink a bit earlier in the mornings, my job was finished, and my youthful fancy had drawn me to thoughts of deck-chairs in the sun. The Orient Line was an old friend of mine; in past years we had swapped many *quids pro quos*, the quids including a voyage to Australia and a cruise to the West Indies, the quos a fair acreage of boxwood. 'Don't you want a few more engravings?' I asked them.

'There's a cabin waiting for you,' they replied.

So, on St Patrick's Day 1954, I stepped aboard the *Orsova* at Tilbury, and soon the white foam was fanning from her bows, and on either side and astern platoons of gulls were escorting us. We met other liners nearing the end of their voyages, we overtook small coastal vessels setting out upon their courses. An officer discussing the weather ran his finger along the teak rail. 'No,' he said, finding it dry, 'I think we'll escape fog.'

That night as I lay in my sumptuous cabin, I thought of the little *barque bleue* in which I had made my last voyage. Eleven feet six inches she was over-all; the *Orsova* was 722 feet 10 inches. I had had but one deck, the bottom of the little boat; the *Orsova* had fourteen. My boat had drawn three inches of water, the *Orsova* needed thirty feet. She'd never have got under those footbridges on the upper Seine.

Next morning the purser inquired if I had been comfortable in my twin-bedded stateroom—'the honeymoon suite,' he called it.

'Only one piece of furnishing lacking,' I told him.

'It's our maiden voyage,' he replied.

During a moment of relaxation on deck I found in the chair next to mine de Lacey Fitzgerald, a man who nearly fifty years before had studied painting with me in Harry Scully's studio in Cork.

'How that man cared for tone!' said de Lacey.

I agreed with him. Drawing, colour, and every other desirable attribute would be added, Scully assured us, if first we got our tones right; he nearly broke our hearts with the relative values in black and white of what we were trying to put down in colour.

'Good at colour but not a great draughtsman,' suggested de Lacey.

I agreed again. Scully had little sympathy for attempts

at precision. 'Don't give yourself away: feel it out,' he would say. He had been caught in the tag ends of Impressionism.

'*You* have travelled a different road,' said de Lacey.

'No good groping,' I said. 'Engraving has taught me that. A stroke should be a stroke, not a fumble.'

We laughed at the memory of how Scully would put us men to draw the cast of Hercules and the women that of the Venus de Milo. A nude model was not to be heard of in Cork. Scully, a Protestant puritan, said it was the fault of the priests; but on the only occasion that I was allowed to draw the Venus, he could not bring himself to mention the word 'breasts,' but explained the significant angles of the hemispheres by dumb gestures.

We were puritanical in those days in Cork. My mother once confided to me that on a visit to London with her husband, my reverend father, they had arranged with two other Cork friends to visit the Royal Academy. Better not wait outside, said one. Let's meet inside, at No. 10 in the catalogue, suggested another—that would be just inside the door. 'And when we got there,' said my mother, 'I didn't know where to look. No. 10 was a naked woman! We couldn't stand in front of that.' How they got over their embarrassment I do not remember.

'In Ireland,' said de Lacey, 'they are suspicious of artists, they have a terror of their morals.'

'In England,' I said, 'they have a fright of their finances. And in France they don't give a damn for either.' Then I told him of how the headmaster of an art school in

London had once said to me: 'We have cleaned up our streets and put our public lavatories underground; now we must clean up our art.'

'What would a Frenchman say to that?' asked de Lacey.

'One of them told me,' I said, 'that it was the funniest remark that had ever come out of England.'

'No wonder their minds are clear to paint,' said de Lacey a trifle sadly.

Of course, art has no more to do with morals than the teaching of a prelate has to do with the shape of his hat. Art is concerned only with intrinsic truth, and how and by whom the price is paid and those truths are purchased and expressed is of secondary importance. Art is the expression of the essence of reality, stripped of all accidental qualities, honest. Picasso's goat in bronze possesses every goatish quality and nothing else; that is why it is so splendid, classic in its analysis of essentials. Abstractions are made from knowledge, not from ignorance.

Gibraltar loomed above us, formidable, every bastion and escarpment of primary importance to those living ashore, yet to us on our way no more than a fragment of a backcloth. Passengers leaving the ship surrendered their personalities as they stepped into the launches; their entities seemed to have dissolved before they reached the shore.

As the ship moved from the harbour and left astern the scene of so much drama, I felt as many do in a train when rushing through the countryside. Looking from the window we see our fellow creatures as midgets in a microcosmic world, and we find it difficult to realize that they too suffer and enjoy; still more so that they, glancing in our direction, should think of us merely as so many gnats in a hurry.

Ogden Nash has combined the two experiences into one coherence:

> '. . . Two beautiful things that are to my mind
>   outstanding,
> And one of them is to be on a train,
>   And see what we see when we flatten our
>   noses against the pane,
> And the other is wistful enough to make any-
>   body feel cosmic and pious,
> Which is to stand beside the track and wave at
>   the passengers as they rocket by us.'

CHAPTER TWELVE

APART FROM arid tracks of former chutes of
lava, there was no hint of malignity from
Vesuvius as the *Orsova* rippled the smooth
Bay of Naples. The great truncated cone
stood there as indifferent to the creatures cultivating its
slopes as to the desolation it had contrived among their
forbears. A car was waiting to take me to Positano, some
fifty miles south along the coast, and as I saw little reason
to linger in the city I was soon away from its streets and
passing fields in which great wide-horned oxen laboured
and farms where, in Virgil's words, 'vines are wedded to
the elm.'

The road led from the level plain into hills whose
ravines and narrow valleys were filled as if with smoke

by the silver grey of olive-trees. Orange groves too, the trees sheltered by light mats of thatch under which the fruit among the dark leaves glowed like golden lanterns in a secret shrine. Then we emerged on to a coastline of wild gorges and precipitous cliffs whose summits were lost in cloud. We travelled midway between sea and sky under vast overhanging rock faces, with only a low and broken wall on the ocean side. Giacomino, the chauffeur, sounded his horn continuously; its echoes suggested the approach of other cars. The road ahead was sometimes vertically above us and sometimes sheer below, so much was it twisted, knotted, and looped, like wet string. Then came vines below vines, domes below domes, and the road shining as a snail's track in plunging descent. Giacomino took a hand from the steering wheel and pointing downwards said: 'Positano!'

Plastered houses, cream coloured, white and rose, were clustered against the hillsides of a horseshoe bay, with steep flights of steps descending at every angle among them. Tiny gardens seemed to straddle rooftops, trees to grow from tiles or chimneys. The end of the road was not quite the end of the journey. In what was hardly more than a courtyard, known as the Piazza, porters were waiting to carry my baggage still further towards the sea, even to the 'Mouth of Bacchus.'

The night before I left England a friend of mine had said to me: 'If you ever get to Positano stay at the Buca di Bacco.' I answered him: 'My baggage is already labelled to that address.'

Quiet, cool, and calm upstairs, a generous ration of local colour at ground level: I never want to stay in a pleasanter hotel. Until a few years ago the residential side of the establishment scarcely mattered: it was the vaulted cellar opening on to the beach that brought the trade. Artists and fishermen congregated there, some to play dominoes or cards at small tables around the central pillar of the room, others to sit on high stools in the alcoved bar. They still do these things to-day, though not on quite the scale that brought the house its name. In those great times there was an artist, a Dane, who had for his breakfast each morning a bottle of brandy and a piece of dry toast; but it is said that he rarely finished the toast. To-day it is the food as well as the wines that epicures seek.

Here at the Buca, looking landwards from my veranda, I found rectangles relieved by arcades and arches—clusters of flat-roofed houses perched one above the other. Such things I had seen in Malta and engraved in black and white nearly forty years before; but now, instead of the cut stone walls of Valetta, Hamrun, and the Citta Vecchia, untouched by artificial stain, the plastered houses shone with every shade of wash, their shadows vivid as they were strong. Doors and windows, more flamboyant, sang emerald and blue or shouted scarlet.

There was colour, too, and pattern when turning from the hills I looked seawards. Fishing-boats on the beach, all shades of green and white, all shades of blue and white, striped the purple sand. Their paint shone: the blues and greens as rich as those in the sunlit water, the whites more dazzling than in the breaking waves. Under a boat, spread-eagled in the shade, lay a fisherman in phlox-pink shirt and turquoise trousers, beside him another in dove-grey shorts, his sunburnt torso more luminous than the sand on which he lay.

In the early morning boats come in from the sea, and men carrying strings of tunny fish in their hands and boxes of smaller fish on their heads walk barefoot across the sand. Sometimes the catch is eels, three and four feet long, fish that swallow the bait deeply and do not die quickly. Rather than extricate the hook through rows of snapping needle-sharp teeth, the fishermen attach it to its line by a snood. As soon as the fish is safely in the boat this is detached and another fitted—it is time enough to recover the hooks when the fish are being cleaned on shore. Larger boats come in from trawling and land great tubs of whitebait or sardines. Then the nets are spread to dry, and as the day advances old women sit on the sand and repair torn meshes.

It was when talking to one of the fishermen that, pointing seawards, I inquired the name of the island that lay some few miles from the shore.

'Sirenuse,' he said, 'the island of sirens.' Then, putting a finger in each of his ears, he said with a significant look: 'Ulysses!'

So this was the island by which the Homeric hero could not pass without stopping the ears of his crew with wax and having himself tied to the mast. The following day I found a boatman who would take me there.

What I had seen from the shore as a single strip of land
turned out to be three separate islands, divided by narrow
channels. The furthest of them was where the girls had
lived, a huge semicircular grotto.

It was a bright day without a breath of wind and the
surface of the water was like the proverbial mirror.
Strangely enough, as we came near to the cliffs, their stone
took on more and more the appearance of human forms.
Looking into the sun and slightly dazzled, I could have
sworn that at any moment those limbs would move, either
to slip into the sea or glide away into the shadows. Indeed, their reflections in the tranquil water were already
moving. And to add to the illusion, I could hear gentle
murmurings and sighings from the caves within the grotto,
as if of human voices. It was easy to see how the myth
had arisen.

I made a drawing of the great shadowed bowl, and another of a smaller cave whose laminated walls deep in the
clear water were heavily encrusted with purple sea

urchins. Then as we turned our bow to the mainland I inquired of the boatman: 'Are there no sirens now?'

'No sirens now,' he said sadly. And then his face lit up. 'But the *signore* of the island is also the *signore* of a great ballet. In the summer when he comes he brings with him many of his dancers.

Les Sylphides have taken over, I thought. 'And they dance in the moonlight?' I suggested.

'I have heard the fishermen say that sometimes when the moon is shining they have seen them dance, and they look beautiful, like white birds. Then afterwards when they dive into the sea they shine silver like fish.'

Looking shorewards, Positano, which from sea level climbs upward eight hundred feet or more, lay like a little heap of white pebbles at the foot of a high cliff, such is the grandeur of the landscape. Landslides that had been major disasters in the lives of the people showed as mere trickles of sand on the mountainside. Vast caverns yawned, toothed with stalactites. Huge pillars of golden rock stood aloof, crowned with green foliage. The road was no more than the scratching of a thorn on a corrugated hide.

As I was stepping ashore my boatman referred to the rough drawings at which he had watched me work. 'You have made a miracle,' he said. 'If I did not see, I would not believe.' Then, as the first drops of a thunder shower fell, he looked up at the sky and shrugged his shoulders. 'What of it?' he said. 'The sun has shone for you this morning, the sea was calm, and you have done the thing you wanted to do. You must sing as you go home.'

It was another man of Positano who said to me: 'When the sun is not shining I must sing to keep my heart warm. When the sun is shining I sing because my heart is warm.'

A fisherman from a neighbouring village who but a few years ago lost his sight attributes his blindness to the sirens. It may be that in his darkness he has dreamed of things that never happened. He tells how one evening in his boat when setting pots for lobsters close to Sirenuse he saw wedged among the rocks at the water's edge a baulk of timber, dark with age. When he went closer, thinking to retrieve it, he could see that below the surface it had the form of a woman's breasts and shoulders, and then he realized that it was the figurehead of some long lost ship. While he looked and pondered, he noticed a glint of light, and peering in he saw beyond the weed-grown figure a lake of blue water lit from below like the grotto at Capri. As his eyes grew accustomed to the dimness he discerned ledges of rock around the blue pool, and on the ledges, shining white as if made of bones, were models of old-time galleys. And suddenly the surface of the pool was broken and two women came up out of the water and their eyes were bloodshot and each had scales on her body from the hips downwards. This so scared the fisherman that he turned and made for the mainland. But he was scarcely clear of the island when he heard voices calling and saw women in the water following him. Strain at the oars as he might, they caught up with him and, as it seemed, were

79

about to take hold of the boat. But instead, one of them cupping her hand threw water into his face. Then they disappeared and he with eyes smarting rowed back to shore. All that night his eyes burned, and when he woke next morning it was as if he was looking through a cloud of smoke. As day succeeded day the cloud thickened, until there came a time when he could see no more. And to-day as he tells the story he is conscious only of a pale-blue light that seems to penetrate his lids, as it were the waters of the grotto shining through the crevice in the rocks.

CHAPTER THIRTEEN

IT WAS SOME few weeks after I had reached Positano that an artist living in the village asked me if I knew of any studio in London where he could shake down for a month or two.

'My place is empty. You can have it if you like,' I said.
'Is mine on the hill any good to you?' he asked.
And so it was arranged.

Seven hundred steep steps from the beach before I tottered against the gate of his vine-canopied terrace. The house had six rooms, three above three, all the lower ones opening on to the terrace. The whitewashed walls were massive, but upstairs the floor beams creaked ominously under the lightest tread. From the windows as from the terrace there was an unbroken vision of sea and sky.

It was quiet in that Olympian abode. Sitting on the terrace in freckled light I could watch small red-breasted finches and white-throated warblers flittering among the

cherry and orange blossoms close below me, or, looking out
to sea, I could descry lateen-sailed craft moving slowly on
the horizon. As I surveyed the wide vista there came to
my memory a day when in an amateur production of the
morality play *Everyman* I played the minor part of God.
The setting was an ancient tithe barn in Wiltshire, considered by William Morris to be one of the most beautiful
buildings in England, and I in sky-blue robe and golden
halo had to declaim through an inside window of a loft
some of the opening phrases of the drama, beginning
slowly and impressively: 'I per-ceive, here, in my maj-
esty. . . .' Some years later I happened to be passing that
farm and, thinking to revisit the scene of the play, I
knocked at the door of the owner's house. Getting no
answer and finding no one near by, I took the liberty of
going through the open door of the barn. The place
seemed empty and I spent some time among the ricks,
seeing again the entries and the exits of the various
characters: Beauty, Good Deeds, Knowledge, and other
abstractions. I had just recognized the little high-up
window behind which I had sat in glory when a sudden
shout asked me in no uncertain terms what I thought I
was doing. I turned to find the owner advancing upon me
angrily. I was about to apologize and explain when he
stopped, took off his hat, and said: 'Why, you're God!
You must come to the house and have some tea.'

That first evening in my new abode, I was searching
for a jam pot or a jug in which to stand my brushes when
a peal of thunder cracked overhead. Looking from the

window I saw that the mountain peaks above the house had disappeared into mist, and from seawards there was approaching an immense bank of streaming purple cloud. It moved steadily towards the land until, as its shadow darkened the white foam at the water's edge, there came a bright flash and another crack of thunder. Then the rain came down 'solid' and gutters overflowed. It was as if vats of water had been spilled on to the roofs. Courtyards became lakes, flights of steps were transformed into torrents.

The rain turned to hail, and almost without ceasing the thunder volleyed in the hills. So for an hour the storm continued, with darkness everywhere. Then, momentarily, the sun shone, and through the break in the clouds thousands of swallows and martins came swirling down. They clung to the stems of trees, to the lattices and pergolas; they clung to the broken plaster under eaves. Almost any of them could have been taken by hand. One came into my kitchen for warmth, lay on a shelf, and did not leave till late next morning. Migrating birds, they had been caught in the storm over Sicily. Two or three days' rest and all but a few continued on their course northwards.

> Nora singing while she scrubs
> Vests and shirts on wooden platter;
> Picking pants from timber tubs,
> Spreading them to drub and batter.
> Chirping encores, while she wrings;
> Birds are mute when Nora sings.

Seventeen-year-old Nora 'went with' the house. She was a powerful girl, as light on her feet on the steep stone stairways as she was heavy with her mallet at the wash-tub in the corner of the terrace. When not barefoot she wore loose sandals whose wooden soles flapped at every step. She could tackle anything, from filleting sardines to placating the plumbing. She took great pride in her work, too, especially her housekeeping. When I told her that she was *molto abile,* mighty clever, she replied that 'one should be able to do anything.' One day having bought from Barbarossa, the red-bearded fisherman, some extra large sardines, she came across the terrace to where I was drawing, holding up one of the fish by the tail. 'Multo grande come Papa,' she said—very big like Papa, the latter for some reason being her term of address for me.

The southern Italians are not of large build and my size often created amusement. Only the day before being likened to a giant sardine, I had visited the Naples Museum and, while awaiting a friend in the entrance hall, had been addressed by three of the uniformed attendants. Where did I come from? they asked. Then each measured himself against me, while others pinched my arms and prodded my chest. Finally all three beckoned that I should follow them, and leading me into one of the main galleries they stopped before an enormous statue of Hercules. 'Simile! Simile!' they said, patting me on the back and pointing to the colossus. For them it was a great piece of fun and we shook hands several times before parting.

Rain or the threat of it made painting out of doors impossible. 'Passion weather,' they called it: it would certainly change on Easter Sunday. But they were wrong. The sirocco continued to blow for weeks after Easter, and everyone became more and more depressed and irritable. 'Now is the time to break the law,' I was told; 'the courts always give light sentences for crimes committed during the sirocco; they accept the wind as mitigation.'

Well, if I couldn't paint out of doors I would try to do so within. I asked Nora to bring me some oranges or some lemons, emphasizing that I wanted them with their leaves on. However beautiful these fruit may be when bare, they are infinitely more so with their foliage. She brought me three oranges and four lemons and put them on a rush-seated chair in my work-room. Would she leave them there? she asked.

'Don't touch them again,' I answered quickly.

Her chance arrangement was perfect. The fruit were clustered there as eggs in a shallow nest, and every rigid line of the chair or its shadow led the eye towards them and their curling leaves.

As I worked I was unconscious of any 'problems' in design or colour: each detail seemed to drop automatically into place, there were no empty spaces, no 'holes.' Only when I had put my brushes down did I realize that I had at last achieved something of that calligraphic quality for which I had been searching. If then I could have got my hand into a position to pat myself on the back, I think I would have done so. Instead, I leaned out of my window for a sniff of evening orange blossom, and just then Monsieur Jean Guyot, an elderly French artist whom I had met while staying at the Buca, pushed open the door of my courtyard. Would I not come down to the hotel that evening? he asked. His car was on the road and he could give me a lift.

Would he not come up and see what I had been doing? I replied. He and I had had many discussions about the problems of an artist's trade as we drank our coffee each morning on the sunlit balcony of the hotel. In particular he had been voluble about the absurdity of students in art galleries copying minutely the works of Old Masters, especially of those with such conspicuous facility of touch as Frans Halz. To follow slavishly all the accidental qualities of his brushwork did not teach the essential fact that such strokes could only have been made after intense observation.

Monsieur Guyot's speech was nicely punctuated, and he had a way of making apposite comments on the work of other painters. Of one who had begun a picture and was not quite sure how he would finish it, he said: 'The artist who hopes for a happy accident to pull him through deserves to die of an unhappy one.' Of another, whose compositions were spoiled by too much adherence to fact, he remarked: 'Reverence for nature too often means irreverence for art.'

As he came into my studio that evening I said to him: 'I *think* I've got going.'

He scrutinized my painting for a while; then, turning to me, he said: 'Monsieur, *vous y êtes*—you've got it.'

What more could I want? 'It's "yes" for the Buca,' I said.

CHAPTER FOURTEEN

ON THE MORNING following my adventure
with the chair and fruit, I explained to Nora
that I did not wish to alter their arrangement
just then but I did want a squeeze of lemon
in my Cinzano. She appeared to understand and tripped
off gaily towards the fruit and china shop on the hill.
When for the second time the outer door had banged and
she came galloping up my stairs, it was with three large
lemons and an orange in her apron. Where should she
put them? she asked, thinking apparently that I was going
to do another painting. I pointed to a stool on which lay
my hat, my white hat from the Pacific. 'Throw it aside,'
I intimated with a gesture. She misunderstood: instead
of moving the hat, she tipped the contents of her apron
into it. When she stepped back there was another composition before me. Again it was as if someone held my
hand. By early afternoon there was nothing more that I
could do to the canvas, and that evening I dealt with a
stray orange on a green saucer—repetitive rings of colour,
rich in shadow and in light.

It is strange how these spasms happen, moments all too
brief when every object before one's eyes seems impatient
for its frame. They don't last long: as a kiss may give

them birth, a cuss may kill them. Then for a while the world is pallid and the mind devoid of motive.

It was during one of these empty intervals that I visited the district west of Naples which, because of its many subterranean and volcanic activities, was known to the ancients as the Phlegrean Fields. Cumae with the Cave of the Sibyl, recently excavated, was my principal objective, but there was also Lake Avernus which at one time provided such an easy descent into the underworld. There it was that Aeneas entered 'the deep yawning cave, sheltered by woodland gloom' and made his way into 'the land of drowsy night,' crossing the river Styx and passing Cerberus and the Furies that he might learn from the shade of his father Anchises the destiny of his race.

The grotto of the Sibyl was not discovered until the summer of 1932. A long dim tunnel carved out of the volcanic rock on the western side of the Cumaean hill, it lies almost immediately under the ruins of the temple of Apollo at which supplicants worshipped before approaching the prophetess. Virgil, after describing the landing of Aeneas on the nearby shore, tells how his hero sought

> '. . . the castled height
> And temple, to the great Apollo dear,
> And the vast cave where, hidden far from sight
> Within her sanctuary dark and drear,
> Dwells the dread Sibyl. . . .'

From that 'castled height' I looked across fields and vineyards to the strand were Aeneas' ships 'with biting anchors' had made fast, and where his youthful followers having come ashore 'sought flints, the seeds of fire.'

How I wished then that I had had an inspiring classics master at school instead of a sad old man who had advertised for a wife and suffered greatly from the answer. The only time I can remember him smiling was after I had handed him my weekly essay, a poem relative to the landing of Aeneas on the banks of the Tiber (*Aeneid,* Book VII):

> The sea was calm, the sun was hot,
> His sailors had perspired a lot:
> Quoth he, Let us make for the shore
> Where we may eat and drink galore.

The next stanza eludes me, but the cadence continues:

> And when at length to shore they'd come
> And when to feast they had begun,
> 'Twas then they found to their disgust
> That all their bread was green with must.

After that my memory fails—which is as well, perhaps.

The vast cave of which the poet Virgil speaks is a gallery some hundred and forty yards in length, sixteen feet in height, and at its lower level eight feet wide. From a few feet above the ground the walls slope inward to a narrow ceiling. Six short lateral galleries allow the evening sun to chequer the already ochreous walls. Recesses on the other side held ritual baths. In the shrine at the far end, where from her throne the priestess pronounced

her oracles, the resonance is such that the quietest spoken
words echo as proclamations, the lightest footfalls resound
as the tread of heavy feet.

Twice I visited Avernus, 'that gloomy lake over whose
pestilent waters no bird could fly unhurt.' Was not the
sulphurous spring upon its shore the outpouring of Styx
itself? On both days that I was there the sky was clear,
and dove-grey terns hovered and dipped above the sunlit
waters. Sandpipers skimmed the surface, and frogs in
their thousands croaked and grunted happily in the red
weed that carpeted the margins. Owing to seismic dis-
turbances the poisonous spring no longer exists. Owing
to man's activity the surrounding forests have disappeared.
In their place are cultivated acres—beans and vines, po-
tatoes and fig-trees.

From Lake Avernus it was but a short walk to the neighbouring Lake Lucrinus, whose shores during the first
centuries B.C. and A.D. were a fashionable health and
pleasure resort of the Romans. Cicero, the Emperor
Vespasian, and Pompey the Great all had their villas beside the lake. So did Agrippina, mother of Nero, until
she was murdered by her son. Agrippina had a double
tooth on the right side of her jaw, which Pliny regarded
as an omen of great destiny. What she did was to produce
Nero. I was once a little anxious about this, because I
also have a double tooth. But I needn't have worried; all
the seven children that I have produced are nice, quiet,
decent creatures. My double tooth is on the left side.

To-day Lake Lucrinus is hardly more than a large pool

where clusters of stakes make breeding grounds for shell-fish. This is all that remains of a wide lagoon that two thousand years ago was famous for its oysters.

All over that promontory to the west of Naples there have been constant changes in land levels, some of them violent, many of them imperceptible in their action. At Pozzuoli, a town on the coast founded in the sixth century B.C., marble pillars in the now waterlogged market-place show by erosion that at one time they were submerged to a depth of twenty feet. Then over a period of centuries they rose above sea level, and now once more they are slowly sinking.

Of the many craters that pock those Phlegrean Fields, that at Solfatara alone, though reticent, is active. Its sandy floor seems but a crust under one's feet, and in its centre a vast vat of mud simmers and splutters. Everywhere in the many-acred expanse stenching fumes issue from innumerable crevices and holes. If only the compulsory guides didn't blather, it would be a place for solemn contemplation.

CHAPTER FIFTEEN

NOT LONG after my visit to Cumae I made my way down to the beach one morning, intending to paint a group of the fishing-boats which usually, for the greater part of the day, are lined up like gulls at the water's edge. But it was Sunday and I had forgotten that on that day all the boats are moved into a huddle elsewhere on the beach so that goal-posts can be erected and a touch-line of rope put down for a football match, nine a side, on the sand. The boats were being shifted when I arrived, and I was watching the heavy work of sliding them yard by yard over runners when I was hailed by three men sitting at their ease in the sun. The artist among them, a short man with black hair, curling beard, and large dark eyes, was lamenting to his companions, a bald-headed financier and a tall, blond philosopher, that he had just sold one of his pictures. 'To sell a picture to a stranger is a sad thing,' he said; 'to give one to a friend is a joy. I did like that canvas, and now I shall never see it again.' Turning to me as I sat down: 'You are wise to be an engraver,' he said; 'you can always keep a copy of what you have done.'

'Most of what I have done,' I said, 'I would gladly destroy. When I was young and needed time for thought, I had no time for thought. Almost everything I did was hurried.'

'Time is money may be true for business men,' said the philosopher, 'but money is time is more true for artists.'

'We are starting a school here,' said the artist, 'which we hope will earn us both money and time.' He took from his pocket a folded leaflet. 'This is a draft of our prospectus,' he said, handing it to me.

From a hurried glance I learned that students were to be offered 'a course' lasting one week of five days, four hours a day, in which they would study drawing, painting, lino cutting, and many other subjects. They would also hear lectures on the Philosophy of Art. If at the end of that week's study they had not imbibed all that they wished to know about Art, they were entitled to a supplementary course of the same duration at a reduced fee and without further entrance fee.

I was struggling for a suitable comment when the financier inquired if any of us knew the current wholesale price of sardines in London. Locally there had been some big catches and he was interested. None of us could oblige.

He was a sad-faced man, able at any moment to impart the price of gold and its backing of paper currency in any country of Europe and in quite a few beyond the seas. That he should be on cordial terms with improvident companions was typical of the tolerance of the heterogeneous population of Positano.

The philosopher inquired of me what I had been doing of late; he had not seen me in the village or on the beach.

'Among other things, Cumae,' I said.

'Ah, you have been seeking advice!' he exclaimed excitedly.

'No,' I said, 'just wandering.'

'But you *should* have sought advice,' he said. 'You should have asked for a dream that would explain yourself. You were in a most evocative atmosphere.'

'The Sibyl is no longer there,' said the artist.

'It does not matter *who* you ask,' answered the philosopher, 'it is the asking, the putting yourself into the right state of mind to receive and understand—that is what is important. A little while ago,' he continued, 'I invoked Mercury, the Messenger, asking him for a dream that would clarify one of my problems. That night I dreamed that I was Micky Mouse riding on a very old thin horse, like Don Quixote's Rosinante. It was bony and underfed but willing, and when it tried to gallop it did so in long slow jumps. And there were twenty or thirty elephants chasing me and it was all happening in a desert.'

Just then some footballers came along, wishing to plant a boat where the four of us were sitting, so we moved to a safe distance from their pitch. There we found ourselves flanked in more senses than one by a number of sun-drowsed beauties who in skin-tight next-to-nothings were lying on the sand, tempting providence and others. Not far away a man was taking a photograph of a young couple standing arm in arm.

'There was a girl lived here before the war with her mother,' said the artist, 'an English girl—very fair, wonderful features. The photographer up in the Piazza did a study of her head, and he framed it and hung it on the wall of his studio. Then the war came, and the girl and her mother had to leave Italy. Later on, there was a rest camp here for English officers, and one of them went along to have his photo taken—he'd had a head wound and he wanted to show his mother that he wasn't scarred. When he saw the girl's picture in the studio he fell in love with it. "Put that in the background of my picture," he told the photographer. Well, his mother was delighted with the result, so was he, and always afterwards he kept a copy in his wallet. Now here's the curious thing. After he'd come out of the Army he was offered a job in Egypt, and when he was on his way there he suddenly felt that he *must* go back to Positano. He couldn't explain why, even to himself, but he hopped his ship at Naples and came down here. On his very first night at the Buca, who should he see sitting on the terrace but the girl in the photograph. She'd come back for a few days to arrange for the sale of her mother's house. He walked across to her table, pulled the photo out of his wallet, and showed it to her. "I've carried that with me for three years," he said.'

'And so they got married?' asked the philosopher.

'And lived happily ever after,' said the artist.

It was getting too hot on the beach for those of us in clothes, so we moved to the terrace of the Buca, interrupting a children's game of marbles played with hazel nuts. I was sorry not to have heard more of the philosopher's dream, but an hour later as he and I plodded up some of the seven hundred steps that led to my house he told me that a friend of his, a colleague of Jung, had given him the interpretation. 'I am ill treating the animal feelings in me,' he said. 'That is the old horse—I am not giving them enough food or freedom. Through their neglect I am starving the mind that carries me. The elephants mean animal wisdom. It is always a very good thing when you dream of elephants.'

He was young and I hadn't the heart to suggest to him that overfeeding of the animal emotions might be as injurious as starvation to the mental processes.

'And you?' he asked, as we paused half-way up for a breather. 'I suppose you're doing some engravings of Positano?'

'Mostly I'm trying to paint in oils,' I said.

'But why not tempera?' he asked. 'It's formal like an engraving. My sister works in that. You'd like it.'

'Yes,' I said, 'but it's to get away from formality that I'm using oils.'

We didn't say much more until we reached my gate. 'Do try tempera,' he urged as he left me.

Another finger-post, I thought as I went in. I find few people more exasperating than those who tell me what I ought to do and how I ought to do it—finger-posts pointing from my own main track to a warren of imitative experiences. An artist may not know his ultimate destination, but only he can see his next step in an untrodden meadow —if the urge and instruction come from outside, the work must of necessity be second hand. It is the same in Academies of Art where as often as not the fires of creation are smothered by the ashes of tradition. Recently a voluble young student complained to me that his school of art was not bringing him all that he wished. 'It is what *you* bring to the school that matters,' I said, whereupon he fell silent.

CHAPTER SIXTEEN

MONDAY MORNING brought a long-awaited cable from Paris: 'Studio on Île St-Louis available from June fifteenth.' Just a fortnight to go.

And following the cable there came another pull at my bell, and Signor Orlando, a local resident, appeared to say that he was taking two English visitors to Paestum and there was a spare seat in his car if I cared to make a four. A few days earlier I had listened to a discussion on the three Greek temples which stand there—one of them 'the most beautiful and best preserved of its kind in the world, bar none—not even excepting the Parthenon.' Signor Orlando, who had been present, had said that he might be going in that direction one day on business and if so he would take me. It was about fifty kilometers to the south from Positano, and after Salerno the road was flat and straight.

The two Misses Elkins, Pam and Dorothy, who awaited us in the car, were twins. Petite, fluffy, and perky, they were like two young birds from the same nest. While Orlando was negotiating with practised ease the acute contortions of the road, he discoursed to us about the places of interest that we passed. There were castles on every headland, 'Saracen towers,' he called them. During the ninth and tenth centuries the Saracens were constantly

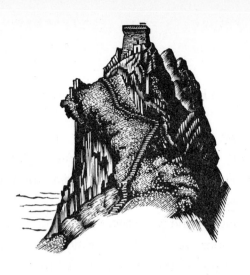

raiding the villages along the coast, carrying off young girls and anything else of value that they could find. So these towers were built, and when the plundering ships were sighted fires would be lit on the flat roofs as signals of danger.

It was from one of these raids that the annual *festa* on 14th August originated. As pirates were breaking into the house of one of the girls, she managed to snatch up a small picture of the Madonna of Positano and hide it in her clothes. Then when she had been carried on board and the ship was moving out to sea, she and the other girls prayed to the Madonna. Suddenly the wind changed and a gale blew them back on shore. So now, on that night of the year, the fishermen build up their boats to look like Arab dhows and they blacken their faces and they come in to the harbour at night and pretend to carry away the young girls. And everyone lets off fireworks to simulate gunfire and then they all pray and then the girls are rescued.

'But is there a special Madonna of Positano?' asked Pam.

'Oh indeed,' answered Orlando. 'You will see her in the church, behind the curtain above the altar. It was she who gave the name to the village. During the time of the suppression of the ikons in Byzantium, about the eighth century, she had been smuggled out of the country and was in a ship making its way along this coast. The weather became stormy and the sailors thought they were finished. Then just when they had given up all hope, they heard a voice from the picture saying, *Posa, posa,* which means put down, put down. So they turned their ship to the shore, and the sea became calm and they were able to land. And that was the beginning of Positano.'

We passed one Saracen tower after another. 'Some day I must make a drawing of one of them,' I said.

'You can do it to-day,' said Orlando. 'There's one just beyond the next corner. It's close to the Santa Rosa convent where I have some business. I'll put you down and come back. How long do you want—half an hour?'

I agreed.

'And there's a nice little café on the side of the road for the girls,' he said. He pulled up as he spoke. The tower stood below us on a high bluff of rock connected to the land by a narrow isthmus. The café was in sight, a hundred yards ahead. The girls said they would explore: Orlando said: 'Back in half an hour—meet you at the café.'

I looked around for the best site from which to make my drawing.

'We're going to inspect the castle,' called Dorothy to me as she and her sister stepped through a gap in the wall that led to a rough track downwards from the road. I watched them for a while as they clambered among the boulders, halting a moment in surprise when a quail rose almost from under their feet, pausing in delight to look at the many species of wild flowers that grew among the stones: small rose-tinted gladioli, tall blue anchusa, tawny snapdragons, clusters of giant rock-roses, bushes of honey-suckle, countless varieties of vetches, scabious, and broom. I could hear them exclaiming at each new surprise of scent or colour. Then their voices died away as they began to climb the steep, zigzag stairway that led to the door of the tower, and putting them out of my mind I began to draw.

It seemed a very short while before I found them back on the road beside me.

'What *do* you think we found in the tower?' asked Dorothy excitedly.

'Coffins!' said Pam, without waiting for my answer.

'Dozens of them, of all shapes and sizes,' said Dorothy.

'Thrown in any old how, like trunks in a lumber-room,' said Pam.

'Were there bodies in them?' I asked.

'They seemed to be empty,' said Pam.

The alternating barrage of words continued.

'Some of them were carved,' said one.

'And some were gilded and some were painted,' said the other.

'And there was a small one, a child's, I suppose, covered in pink satin, torn and faded.'

'There was another room above but we couldn't get into that—the door was wired up,' said Pam.

'But I could see a coffin in there too,' said Dorothy.

'Give me five minutes to finish this drawing and I'll meet you at the *trattoria*,' I said.

Fifteen minutes later Orlando joined us in the white-washed bar of the inn. What did the coffins mean? the girls asked him. He did not know, but he inquired of the proprietor.

The tower had been used as a cemetery until a few years ago, we learned. It was hard to dig a grave in the rocky ground so it had been the custom, after the funeral service, to place the coffin in the upper room of the tower and to leave it there for a reasonable period—perhaps two years. Then relatives would put the bones into a small box which they placed in a hole in the wall of the tower, and the empty coffins were thrown into the lower room, where the *signorinas* had found them.

Seeing a small woven basket containing two faded sprays of leaves hanging on the wall, I inquired if they were the holy palm from Easter. The daughter of the house, a girl of about fifteen with a mass of dark hair hanging over her shoulders, answered no, that they were olive leaves. 'It is the olive that is blessed in southern Italy,' she said. Was it not on the Mount of Olives that Jesus suffered? Was it not a branch of olive that the dove brought to Noah after the Deluge?

Orlando had come back merely to tell us that he had to pay a short visit to a neighbouring vineyard. 'Why not do a drawing of the convent while you are waiting?' he suggested. 'There's a fine view of it from the road.'

'We'll walk on slowly,' said the girls, as I sat down on my stool and began to do as I'd been told.

An hour later we were all together again and continuing our journey through tunnels, over bridges, and round a succession of loops to Amalfi, Maiore, and Minori, each of their beaches gay with bright umbrellas and rows of striped bathing-huts.

At Vietri we paid a brief visit to one of its many pot-teries—for the most part small family affairs. In this particular workshop grandfather, father, and son were all at their wheels, close to the great vats of clay in their yard. Upstairs other members of the family were decorating the finished clay with traditional designs. Times beyond computation the same pairs of hands had painted the same patterns in the same colours, yet there was no trace that I could see of the faults of mass production. A good actor is as good at the thousandth performance as he is at the first; these painters dropped their designs on to vase or platter as lightly and surely as a dancer treads a well-known measure.

After Vietri, Salerno with its grim beaches: then the mountains dropped away and low gentle hills formed the background to a wide cultivated plain through which the road stretched straight and flat.

Drink wine of the country; read, verse of the country. How much better scans Mallarmé in that forest by the Seine: how much better sound the Georgics where steers still lumber at the plough. Virgil, the poet of 'tilth and vineyard, hive and horse and herd,' counselling the mother-suckling of young calves:

'Nor, as our fathers did, shall you allow
The nursing dams to fill the snowy pail;
Nay! give their pretty sons an udder-full.'

Could any words be more evocative of the warm sweet

smell of cows and nuzzling calves and splashing milk? It
was of these fields, too, that he advised

> 'So ply your hoes and give the weeds no peace,
> Scare birds with noise, correct the leafy hedge
> Too lavish with its shade, pray hard for rain.'

He goes on to speak of ploughshares and threshing floors,
of choice of seed, of spring sowings, summer ripenings and
autumn reapings, of winter when

> '. . . 'tis time
> To strip the oak of acorns and the bay
> Of berries, and to gather olive fruit
> And blood-juiced myrtles.'

His words ring just as true to-day, of wheat and barley,
oats and beans, olives and trellised vines.

In places the road was lined with poplars, so pollarded
that their branches met overhead. We travelled through
green tunnels, the air thick with the white fluff of their
pollen. Drifts of it lay on either side. I noticed small
herds of buffaloes in marshy fields. 'Their milk is good
for cheese,' said Orlando. We passed high-wheeled carts,
brightly painted in traditional patterns, drawn by a horse
or mule in double harness with a tiny donkey.

There is no need for hill or acropolis at Paestum. Here
on this plain in unobtrusive splendour have stood for
2,500 years these monuments to perfection. Here, at last,
in these temples everything is right, everything is fitting.

There is no need to wonder at the idiosyncrasies of architects, to ask why Palladio did this or Wren did that. No single stone could be moved without detriment to the whole. The whole is as a single stone. In each of the three buildings the absolute has been attained.

During the seventh century B.C., the Greek colonists then occupying southern Italy founded the city of Poseidonia on the shores of the Gulf of Salerno, naming it in honour of the sea god. Four centuries later the newly arisen power of Rome drove out the Greeks, and in their place established the Latin colony of Paestum which, thanks to its trade in the oil and cereals produced in the surrounding plain, flourished for many centuries. But gradually, owing to changes in the level of the coast, here as at Pozzuoli and elsewhere, the mouth of the river Salso, on which the town was built, silted up and the whole coastal area changed from fertile land to swamp; and from the swamp came malaria. By the tenth century the few surviving inhabitants had fled to the mountains and the deserted city became lost in marsh and forest. Even the memory of its existence perished. Not till the eighteenth century was the site of the city rediscovered.

The three temples dominate all else. Around them are the foundations of altars and of fountains, the pillars of a forum, the tiers of seats in an arena, the broad paving-stones of sacred ways, fragments of statues, of cornices and mouldings. They are but a filigree setting. As the hosts of birds that hive among the metopes and niches of the pediments, as the flowers that sing in unison from every cranny, so are these crumbs of stone.

When the monuments were rediscovered, names were given to them which though still in use are now considered erroneous. That to the south, of which I have drawn a fragment, is the oldest of the three, dating from the middle of the sixth century B.C.; it was thought to be a civic rather than a religious building and became known as the Basilica. Like its more noble neighbour, the 'Temple of Neptune,' it was dedicated to Hera, goddess of fertility, a fact proved by inscriptions on fragments of vases found during recent excavations. Likewise, heads and other pieces of small statuettes indicate that the 'Temple of Ceres' was in fact raised in honour of Athena, goddess of Wisdom and protectress of agriculture, who invented the rake and bridle and taught the people to yoke oxen to the plough. On the day of my visit, a reaping-machine drawn by two milk-white oxen was cutting the wild wheat and barley that grew around her shrine.

The Temple of Neptune, of massive dignity and grace, is the largest of the three sanctuaries. Close on two hundred feet in length and eighty wide, its fifty-eight columns, convex as muscles swelling under strain, have mellowed to the tints of saffron and cinnamon, and at sunset the building seems aflame.

A strange contrast, these solitary legacies of grandeur, with the trivia of daily life found and still to be seen in the not far distant ruins of Pompeii and Herculaneum. The sudden tragedy of those buried towns is epitomized in the piece of bread on a larder shelf, a woman's trinkets scattered on a table, dishes of beans and cereals on a shop counter. Most poignant the mould of a chained dog in its last tortured moments. The horror of the scene comes to us in the well-known letter of Pliny the Younger, who was an eye-witness of the disaster.

'And now cinders which grew thicker and hotter fell into the ships, pumice grit, too, and stones blackened and cracked by fire. Then, of a sudden the sea ebbed from under them and the shore became blocked by landslides from the hills. . . . On the other side a black and awesome cloud burst into gusts of fiery serpentine vapour, and at intervals yawned open to reveal long capricious flames. . . . Darkness came upon us, not like the darkness of a moonless night or one with cloud but rather of a room with the lamp extinguished and closely shut. You could hear the screams of the women, the cries of the children, and the shouts of the men, some of them praying to die from the mere fear of dying, others lifting their hands in supplication to the gods, the greater part imagining that the gods had forsaken them and that the everlasting night had come upon the world.'

Where life ceased as abruptly as light at the pinching of a candle, we find a picture of the distant past; but at Paestum, though for centuries deserted, we find a living beauty.

CHAPTER SEVENTEEN

ON MY LAST night in Positano I dined at the Buca, and after darkness had fallen clattered homewards up the hill in a *carrozza*. Wisps of cloud silvered by an unseen moon looped from mountain peak to mountain peak. The sky above them was thickly starred and, as if to challenge their light, innumerable fireflies glowed from either side of the road. The candle in the one lantern of the vehicle made no impression on the darkness. Dimly lit archways hung in space above our heads.

Farewell to Positano! Farewell to those pillared hills above me, time-worn palaces of ancient gods; to the seven hundred knee-cracking steps below me, to the people who rejoice in the sun and take life as it comes. I thought of one of them who had assured me of fine weather for a proposed expedition; his forecast proved wrong—it poured the whole of the day. When I met him next morning, he smiled and shrugged his shoulders. 'Well, what of it?' he said. 'Was it not good also to have a day of quiet in the house—to read and to think? And did you not sleep well in your bed last night? And look, the sun is now shining.'

Giacomino the taxi-driver had many virtues, in particular that of punctuality; and knowing that it might perhaps be my last journey along that road to Naples he was thoughtful enough on the morning of my departure to be at my gate half an hour before the appointed time. 'We drive *piano,* then you admire,' he said in explanation.

As we loaded my baggage into the back of the car a man came trotting down the hill with a couple of bags of cement thrown across his shoulders: the two-hundred-weight that he was carrying did not prevent him waving gaily as he passed. Barbarossa, with a wide basket of fish balanced on his head, came up the hill calling '*Pes-ce!* *Pes-ce!*' Nora thought it very funny to see two men with beards shaking each other by the hand.

As we drove along the coast road, gnarled and twisted as a vine stem, we could see across the water first the low arcades of Sirenuse and then the precipitous facets of Capri. Giacomino asked if I had been to that latter island.

'Once,' I said.

'You like it?'

'Once was enough.'

'Many visitors?'

'Too many,' I answered.

One day there had certainly been enough. The historical and romantic interests of the island are hidden behind a façade of artificiality. Exploitation of tourists seemed the basic idea of most of the inhabitants; exposure of their anatomy that of most of the visitors. Of what possible use is a Bikini to a woman of fifty with a waist of forty? But during my few hours ashore one brief incident redeemed the day. With a party of five others I lunched at a restaurant whose terrace overlooked a blue pool, with rustic bridges leading to cunningly devised islets. The food was excellent, the pale Capri wine admirable: the *padrona* herself, who spoke perfect English, supervised our needs. But it seemed to me and, by their glances, to the others too that I was getting special attention. Little extras were quietly manœuvred in my direction, my glass was more frequently filled. After lunch I thought to thank her for this care. 'It is I who have to thank you,' she said. 'I have all your books. Whenever I am sad I read one of them.'

'Praise is the best diet for us, after all,' said Sydney Smith. That day on Capri it made a wonderful digestive.

The train pulled out from Naples. It was hard to believe that I had only to sit where I was, eat and sleep, and in twenty-four hours I would be hearing porters rhyming baggage with barrage rather than with seraglio or cabbage.

> Roma, Livorno,
> Pisa, La Spezia,
> Rapallo, Genova,
> Modane.

The names of the towns through which the train passes —a poem in themselves, yet mighty little poetry in their stations. Quietly and casually, as if it were an everyday affair—which, though hard to believe, it is—the engine-driver brings his rolling stock to a halt between low platforms. No bands, no fanfares of whistles: you might as well be entering Balham on British Railways on a Sunday. I've seen more excitement at Limerick Junction in the old days when two trains were passing than I did from my international express when it paused at Rome, Rapallo, and Genoa.

Limerick Junction, on the main railway line between Cork and Dublin, is an important and ever-growing station. It was when I was a boy that with the increasing traffic on the branch line to the west it became necessary to engage an extra porter, a man who when the trains came in would walk up and down the platform calling out: 'Change here for Sligo, Galway, Mayo.' When on his first tour of duty he moved among the crowds you could hardly hear his voice; he was shy and there were scores on the platform and dozens in the carriages. There was developing a danger that people going west might be going south, and vice versa. So the station master ran after the recruit. 'What are you frightened of?' he asked. 'Sing it out, man,' he said, 'sing it out *loud*!' A few moments later passengers heard, in a rich baritone voice:

'Sweet dreamland faces, passing to and fro,
Change here for Sligo, Galway, and May-o!'

I am sorry that I cannot indicate the correct modulations, but my renderings tend to vary; the emphasis anyway is on the final o.

From Limerick to the power of Ancient Rome. In the year 53 B.C., Julius Caesar appointed the town of Lutetia to be the meeting-place of deputies from conquered Gaul. It was then the capital of the Parisii, an insignificant Gallic tribe who had fortified a small island in the river Seine. To-day that island is known as the Île de la Cité and the city that has grown up around it is called Paris. And I, having left behind me Caesar's Villa, within sight of Lake Lucrinus, was on my way to the Île St-Louis, the sister isle that almost touches the prow of the ancient settlement. I did not then know that from the windows of my studio I would look across to the spires of Notre Dame rising above the oldest quarter of Paris.

CHAPTER EIGHTEEN

THERE WERE ten days before I could get into the studio, so on arrival, by way of a change from the left bank, I went to a small hotel on the other side of the river, not far from one of the ancient gates of the city, the Porte St-Denis. It was quiet there and the room was large enough for an easel as well as a bed. When the weather was fine I pottered about the streets, making odd notes in pencil or in colour. When it was wet I wandered in the galleries.

In the Musée Guimet I saw sculptures from Cambodia, Buddhas with eyes closed, smiling serenely, to whom centuries are as days, calm, kindly, comprehending. Near to them Buddhas from Siam, in bronze, with eyes open, supercilious, disdainful. In the Petit Palais I found the portrait by Toulouse-Lautrec of his father, 'Alphonse de Toulouse-Lautrec-Monfa conduisant son mail-coach à Nice, 1880,' in which the noble parent might well be Don Quixote on the box seat instead of in the saddle. There were also paintings by Daumier, who in his many engravings established the difference that sometimes is apparent between law and justice.

At the Musée d'Art Moderne I would go first to that long gallery where the exuberance of Vlaminck on one side contrasts with the cold disdain of Derain on the other, and both are crowned at the far end by the fierce religion

116

of Rouault. Rouault as a boy was apprenticed to a worker in stained glass and his painting has never lost the strong contour lines and the fiery glints of that medium. Its intensity is alarming until one discerns behind it a great and gentle compassion for suffering humanity. The biographer and art critic Marcel Brion did not exaggerate when he wrote: 'His clowns are the saints, his prostitutes the martyrs of a world where despots and judges tramp heavily on iron-shod feet. In his *Miserere* all the stages of the Passion are carried to the very limits of human suffering. No painter, perhaps, since Giotto, has given us so clearly the feeling that God is man, and that many are the secret, captive, and wounded gods who bleed within man's heart.'

Strange contrast to Rouault, the work of Dufy fills a nearby room. When for the first time you see these apparently flippant superimposings of line and colour you may wonder at their slightness, their casualness; but if then for a moment you close your eyes you will see within your lids the essence of the scene depicted. Dufy is a master of the art that gives to a carefully planned painting the semblance of complete spontaneity.

'There are as many ways of painting as there are painters, though the problem is always the same.' From Dufy one moves to the cubit Braque, who proclaims: 'An idea first. Then begins the adventure which is born under the brush. The idea in a painting is as the scaffolding in a shipyard that is dislodged when the vessel is finished. A picture is finished when the idea has disappeared.'

Thence to the gay 'scholarly artlessness' of Matisse, who said: 'I wish that man, tired and overworked, may find before my pictures calm and repose.' In the next room Picasso. 'We all know,' said the Spanish master, 'that Art is not Truth. Art is a lie that makes us realize truth. The artist must know the manner whereby to convince others of the truthfulness of his lies.' When Henry James spoke of altering facts to create truth, he meant the same thing in literature.

In the annexe to the Louvre, the Jeu de Paume, the atmosphere is more restful. For enjoyment of the ballet girls of Degas or his women in their bath tubs, little mental struggle is needed. Similarly with the glowing portraits and the sunlit children of Renoir. 'I think I am still making progress,' said the old man, when at the age of seventy-eight he lay dying.

English painters since Turner and Constable have not ranked high in France, yet each time I went to that gallery of Impressionists I felt more and more the quiet strength of Sisley, the only Englishman among them; in particular his two canvases of *Inondations à Marly* and his *St Mammès*. Monet, the Frenchman, of greater repute, seemed less and less satisfying, so full of colour yet so lacking in composition. 'I wish to paint as a bird sings, spontaneously,' he said. But then, as someone else said, 'a bird cannot compose a symphony.' In his work there is the joy and lightness of bird song, but there is little of the structural perfection that we find in Manet.

Manet's *Le Fifre,* a boy wearing military uniform that is much too big for him and playing a flute, and his *Olympia,* a pale, naked girl on a satin bed with a negress bringing her flowers, are both well known, but perhaps it is not so well known that Manet painted both from the same model. The soldier boy whom the artist had seen on the barrack square did not turn out to be as good a model as he had hoped. The boy had no idea of keeping the pose and quickly became bored. Manet got more and more irritated until eventually he told him to go home. But Victorine Meurend, Manet's favourite model, who had been mending the artist's socks, came to the rescue. 'Go behind that screen and take off your clothes,' she said to the boy. 'Wrap yourself in this,' she said, throwing him a shawl. Then when the boy had undressed she took his clothes and put them on herself. The next time Manet looked towards the throne it was Victorine that he saw in uniform, and she *was* holding the pose.

Toulouse-Lautrec was thirty years younger than Manet, and one evening some years after the elder man had died, as Lautrec sat at a café in Montmartre, an old woman, bent and shrivelled, approached him selling flowers. He bought a few blossoms, and in his own gracious way thanked her for offering them to him.

'Either you are a great gentleman or a great artist,' she said. 'Only one or the other would have spoken to poor folk like that.' Then she lifted her head and said proudly: 'But I was a friend of a great artist. His name was Manet. I posed for *Le Fifre* and for *Olympia.*'

It would seem that Lautrec did not lose touch with her, for the novelist Paul Leclercq relates that one day after he had been sitting for his portrait to Lautrec the artist said to him: 'Come with me and we will pay a visit.'

'Whom will we visit?' asked the writer.

'Come with me,' said Lautrec.

They went together to a house in one of the poorer quarters of Paris where in a room on the sixth floor they found a little old woman huddled by a stove.

'Allow me to present to you the original *Olympia,*' said Lautrec.

CHAPTER NINETEEN

RAIN! From drizzle to downpour and then again to drizzle. It was impossible to work out of doors and, for lack of daylight, it was impossible to work in my room. It occurred to me that a theatre or a circus might provide a subject. The Concert Mayol, one of the smaller music-halls, was quite near by; I would go and see what was happening. There might by chance be a matinée.

I arrived about three o'clock in the afternoon to find the doors closed to the public and workmen in the foyer putting up a publicity display for a new revue entitled *Ça c'est du Nu*. Well, there should be possibilities in that, I thought, as I turned to go home. But a sudden torrent of rain halted my steps and I sheltered awhile in the vestibule. As I waited a stout and genial-looking man came from inside. Seeing the rain he too stopped. He was wearing a red-and-green pullover, corduroy slacks, and an old felt hat. I took him to be a member of the house. In answer to my inquiry he told me that the new show would open next day—they were now busy on the final rehearsals. The company had gone out for lunch, but he was expecting them back at any moment.

He spoke with an air of authority, and I ventured to tell him what I had hoped to do.

'But you shall draw the rehearsal,' he said.

Just then a party of about a dozen men and women rushed through the rain from a café on the other side of the street and joined us. My friend introduced me, saying that I was an artist about to make drawings of the *répétition*. I shook hands with the author of the new revue, with the *secrétaire général* of the theatre, with the designer of the *décor*, and met also one of the actors with his wife, a former Venus, now an usherette, and most important of all, the star *nu*, with her husband who played the accordion in the orchestra. Then we all passed through the foyer and into the theatre.

Even as a small theatre it was small: there seemed no more than a score of rows, with about six seats on either side of the centre gangway. A ring of low boxes surrounded the stalls, and above them a balcony. Mirrors at the back of the stage-side boxes repeated the scene on the stage.

Dust sheets covered the stalls, but chairs and a table in the aisle awaited the directors. Where would I like to sit? they inquired. I chose a seat in a box about half-way back, where I could work without getting in their way. By now I had discovered that my stout friend was not only the principal comedian of the company but the director of the theatre as well, none other than Paul Ensia. He was also uncle of Monsieur René, the designer. Everyone there seemed to be related.

The orchestra of five was already practising. Scene-shifters were experimenting with fragments of sets. A cardboard wheelbarrow full of painted flowers was let down from above the stage and raised again; two large butterflies were treated in a similar manner. A flight of stairs was unfolded in the centre of the stage and then folded again and taken away. A bath and some mirrors were carried on and off. An elderly woman crossed the stage carrying an armful of tinsel.

Then the scene-shifters let down a backcloth on which was painted a pirate ship and a drop-curtain with a hole in it to represent the mouth of a cave. Pirate girls whose wide hats and tall boots were the most generous parts of their attire began to appear on the scene and stand in groups chatting. The secretary went to his table and began to make notes; the author threw back a corner of a dust sheet and took a front row seat in the stalls. The orchestra fell silent.

All was ready to begin, and to the chords of a West Indian rumba the curtains parted. There were the pirate girls posed around a large open coffer, toying with strings of pearls. But the grouping wasn't to the author's satisfaction. He called to them to do this and then to do that; only after he had himself gone on to the stage and shifted them about as if they were lay-figures did he get the arrangement that he wished.

Next appeared the pirate king, a male dancer. His entry was not quite so dramatic as it should have been, and again the author had to leave his chair and demonstrate. There followed pirate dances to Hungarian folk music, with Les Mayol Pin-up Girls as living pearls. Eventually author, director, and artist approved the sequence, the secretary made a few notes, and the next item was called for. It was a solo dance put on chiefly because it needed little space on the stage and a drop-curtain enabled the next scene to be set while it was in progress. Nobody gave it much attention.

Other items followed, whose titles are self-explanatory: *Pin-up Bar, La Parade d'Amour, Les Nus en Fleurs.* Then came what was to be the act of the evening. The curtains opened to reveal a snow-white bath before a tailor's delight of mirrors. I could hear a rumbling sound, as of mechanism, coming from inside the bath and soon I saw billowing foam. It piled itself, shimmering, a foot above the rim. Everybody was delighted.

The plot of this drama was not difficult to follow. A lady, blonde as a lily, sumptuously dressed, assisted by a negress maid—dark for contrast—had to undress and step into the bath. Nothing could be more modest, the foam was all-concealing. It began beautifully and continued exquisitely till—stop! stop! the girl was taking off her stockings too quickly. It was explained to her that the tension in the audience must be prolonged. On went her clothes and the whole thing began again. This time everything was auspicious until the moment when only one wisp of gossamer remained between the epidermis and the foam. That wisp did not fall; the girl, instead of nipping into the bath, remained seated on her rose-pink stool. When Monsieur Ensia questioned her, she shook her head. When the author called to her through his megaphone, she answered in the same way. Some serious misunderstanding seemed to have arisen. Author, secretary, and designer joined Monsieur Ensia on the stage to reason with her.

At last she spoke and I could hear her firm reply: she would not get into that foam. She had decided that it would be bad for her skin, and her skin was valuable to her.

I came from my box to speak with Monsieur René.

'It is mad,' he said. 'It is the same foam that was demonstrated at the Foire de Paris. It is quite harmless to any skin.'

Then followed much discussion among the others, during which an acrobatic dancer from South America, snatching a moment on the unused stage, nearly broke her neck on the unused bath. The foam subsided.

'Eh bien!' said the director, 'If she is afraid for her skin there are others with more courage.' He called for a volunteer. Not one came forward. The skins of the Pin-ups were equally valuable to their owners.

Consternation followed. Discord had come into the family. The author sat in his front row stall with his head in his hands. 'It would have been the best item in the show,' he groaned.

Wisely, someone suggested that a break for dinner might be opportune.

'How late will you carry on?' I asked Monsieur René, as I followed him through the half-closed exit grille.

'Till morning, probably,' he replied.

Harmony had been restored when, towards ten o'clock,

I returned to my place. A heroine for the suds had been found, and already they were busy with a new item, *Salome 1954:* the programme was nothing if not consistent.

I felt that already I had learned something, if only that the correct unfastening of a suspender belt required the concentration of so many creative minds. But towards two o'clock in the morning I began to feel sleepy. They were working on *Les Bas-Fonds de Paris,* an apache melodrama in which a girl though stabbed mortally manages to keep on her feet until the clamour has subsided and the police gone on their way. I had made a number of drawings and this particular subject did not encourage further efforts. The repetition caused by such details as the snatching of a knife from where there should have been a garter if apache women had not ceased to wear stockings, was making me more and more drowsy. There was trouble too with the lighting, and the girl had to die repeatedly while the electricians made efforts to focus the baleful blue spotlight. It was after many stabbings and dyings that I slipped quietly from my place, made my way into the dimly lit foyer, and sought the street. Alas, the outer doors were shut and the grille locked. Oh well, I thought, I'll have a penn'orth on the house and go back and see it through. In the poor light I could just make out the necessary sign pointing upstairs. I followed the fingers and, as I could find no switches for the lights, I used one of my last two matches to distinguish between *Hommes* and *Dames.* While in the inner sanctum I thought I heard a footstep. What of it? It was probably in the next house.

My last match brought me back to the door, and gratefully I gripped the handle. But the door didn't open. The key had been turned. I was locked in. That footstep must have been the night watchman on his rounds. So there was my saintly self locked in the *cabinet de toilette* of a French music-hall at two o'clock in the morning. It was pitch-dark and I saw no chance of getting out before the following afternoon when the house would reopen.

Without much hope of being heard I shouted for help and kicked as hard as I could at the door. There was no answer. I kicked again, and shouted even louder. Then I heard a voice, and footsteps coming closer. A gleam of light shone under the door. Next moment a platoon of men, headed by Paul Ensia, were staring at me in astonishment. When I told them what had happened they all burst out laughing.

'It is the best turn of the evening,' said Ensia.

'We thought it was a real murder,' said René the artist.

'We'll have it in the next revue,' said the author.

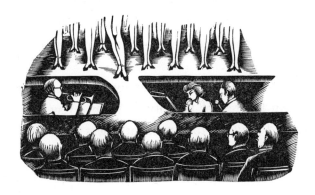

CHAPTER TWENTY

ON THE 15th June I packed my baggage into a taxi. 'You are a painter, then!' commented the driver, as he took my easel from me. He inquired if I had done much work while in Paris.

'Not yet,' I said. 'I've only just got a studio.'

'Montmartre or Montparnasse?' he asked.

'Neither,' I said. 'Île St-Louis, Quai de Bourbon, 53.'

'Ah, l'Île St-Louis!' he exclaimed. 'C'est quelque chose ça—le rêve de bien des gens!'—that is indeed something, everybody's dream.

The inhabitants of the island live as in a garden, set apart from the rest of the city. When a few days after my arrival I inquired for a resident, I was told that he had gone to Paris for lunch. As soon as it was realized that

I had come to live on the Île and was not a passing visitor, I was treated as one of the family. The woman in the *alimentation générale* would pick special fruit for me from deep on her shelves. Even in the wine shops there was no need to pay for anything until I felt inclined. Why yes, there had always been artists living on the Île, many writers and poets too. I soon found myself carrying oddments of stale bread to Madame in the newspaper shop —she had so many to feed, seven cats and five dogs.

Although the Île St-Louis lies so close to the oldest quarter of Paris, it was not until early in the seventeenth century that its character changed and, instead of providing only grazing land for cattle and a site for occasional duels, it became a residential area as fashionable then as it is sought after to-day. Until 1630 what is now one island was divided into two by a narrow branch of the Seine, that portion to the west and nearest to the Cité and its cathedral being known as the Île Notre-Dame, and the other half where cows were pastured as the Île aux Vaches. Then in that year Louis XIII confirmed letters patent to three of his state officials to develop the island. Their names survive in the Pont Marie, one of the bridges connecting with the mainland, and the Rue Le Regrattier and Rue Pouletier, two of the three streets that cross the island from north to south. All round the shores mansions were built for personages connected with the court, and to-day as many as not of the houses on the river fronts bear plaques commemorative of distinguished inhabitants. The island became known as l'Île des Seigneurs: in No. 3

Quai d'Anjou lived the chief architect to the king; in No. 5 the designer of the hydraulic machine that carried water from the Seine to Versailles. No. 9 was inhabited by the Treasurer of State, later by the artist Honoré Daumier.

On the Quai de Bourbon, close to No. 53, there had lived one of the twelve hautboy players to the king; the private accountant to the king; a captain of the Queen's Regiment; and, in a different stratum of society, the daughter of the cabaret proprietor at No. 1, Cécile Renault, who was guillotined for having tried to assassinate Robespierre. The door and window grilles with vine leaf traceries still decorate her house.

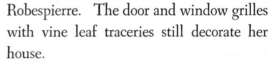

No. 17, Quai d'Anjou, the Hôtel de Lauzun, formerly the Hôtel Pimodan, still keeps its green and gold drain pipes rich with spewing dolphins. Here Baudelaire lived for two stormy years with his Creole mistress, Jeanne Duval. His apartment was on the topmost floor, under the mansard roof, and he had muffled all but the upper panes of the windows so that looking out he saw only clouds. The rooms were small but furnished with enormous arm-chairs and divans. His writing-table was lacquered: on his walls were paintings, engravings, and Japanese prints. No books were visible, his library being hidden in cupboards. Much of the bric-à-brac that filled his rooms had been acquired from a dealer in antiques whose showroom was on the ground floor and who was so accommodating to distinguish clients such as Baudelaire that on one occasion he lent the poet four thousand francs on signature for a mere twelve thousand.

This house became the property of a wealthy book lover who installed there *le club des Hachichins* where Baudelaire, Balzac, Théophile Gautier, and others gathered to smoke opium and chew hashish. Gautier, in an article published in the *Revue des Deux Mondes* in February 1846, tells of his first visit to these monthly meetings. It was about six o'clock on a night in December, wet and cold, when after knocking several times at the outer door he was admitted by a crone who with skinny finger pointed his way across the courtyard. Lights from small square-paned windows guided his steps: long grass growing between the paving-stones wet his feet. Inside the inner doorway he found himself at the foot of an immense staircase such as they constructed in the time of Louis XIV. Its grandeur of proportion and decoration made him feel that in his dull, black coat he ought to have used the servants' stairs. Eventually he entered a large room lit at its far end by lamps, and because of its furnishings it seemed to him as if he had gone back two centuries in time; it was as if the clock had been stopped and nothing had since been altered. He moved towards the lights and was greeted by men seated at a table. 'It is he, it is he,' they cried. 'Let him have his portion!' One of them, referred to as 'the doctor,' then took a morsel of *pâté*, greenish in colour, from a crystal vase and served it to him on a small saucer of Japanese porcelain. As he did so his face glowed, his cheeks grew red, his nostrils dilated. 'These hours will be deducted from your time in Paradise,' he said to Gautier.

After each one had eaten his portion, coffee was served in the Arabian manner—with the grounds left in and no sugar. Then they took their places for dinner. It seemed odd to Gautier that coffee was served before instead of after the meal. The appointments of the table were in every way bizarre. No two plates were alike, some were from China or Japan, others from Limoges or Gascony; the wine-glasses were from Venice or Germany. A philistine might well have been alarmed at the sight of the guests, long-haired, bearded or strangely shorn, brandishing the ancient daggers, Malayan kris, or Spanish poniards with which they ate their food.

Towards the end of the repast, Gautier experienced a complete change in his sense of taste. The water that he drank was like the most exquisite wine. Meat in his mouth tasted of raspberries: he couldn't have told the difference between a cutlet and a peach. Then his neighbours seemed to him to become changed in their appearance. Their eyes grew big and round as those of owls, each man's nose enlarged into a proboscis, faces took on strange colours. Gautier felt spasms of heat in his limbs and waves of dementia passing through his brain.

'To the salon, to the salon!' cried one of the guests. 'Do you not hear the celestial choirs? The musicians await us.' Forthwith the company moved to an adjoining room, enormous, with carved and gilded panels and a painted ceiling. Gautier, seeing a low chair beside the huge marble fire-place, sat in it and gave himself up to the hallucinations that were now crowding upon him. It seemed to him then that one by one his companions disappeared, leaving no more than their shadows on the wall. Solitude reigned: candles innumerable lit themselves. The furnishings of the room became more and more sumptuous. Though he could see no one he could divine the presence of a multitude, he could hear the rustle of clothes, the tapping of shoes, whisperings and hints of stifled laughter.

Suddenly a stranger appeared. Whence he came it was impossible to say. His nose was hooked like the beak of a bird; his eyes, which he was constantly wiping with an enormous handkerchief, were green. In the folds of a high starched cravat he carried a visiting-card—'Daucus-Carota, du Pot d'Or.' His hunch-backed, pigeon-breasted body was covered by a black square-tailed coat. His legs were a root of mandragora, bifurcated, black, rough, full of knots and warts, which seemed to have been but recently pulled from the earth as lumps of soil still clung to the filaments. The little legs wriggled and twisted with tremendous activity, and when the creature came face to face with Gautier he broke into sobs, and in the most miserable of tones said: 'To-day we must die of laughing.' Then looking towards the ceiling Gautier saw a crowd of heads without bodies, like those of cherubim, with expressions so jovial and so happy that he himself could not help joining in their laughter.

Little by little, the room filled with strange figures, tawdry forms half human, half bestial. As if Gautier were king of the festival, each of them came to him in turn and muttered in his ear witticisms which at the time seemed to him deliriously funny but of which afterwards he could remember not a single word. Such hilarity came upon them all that the very floors and walls seemed to shake with the frenetic laughter. Every character invented by mocking sophistry was there, freed of their trammels: the Neapolitan Pulcinella was smacking playfully the hump of the English Punch; Harlequin rubbed his black snout against another's powdered face; Gilles, the French clown (so exquisitely portrayed by Watteau), was kicking the bottom of a Spanish braggart. Others danced dances such as had not been seen even at the time of the Renaissance. Daucus-Carota performed prodigies of pirouettes and other capers on his legs of mandragora, all the time wiping his eyes and repeating: 'To-day we must die of laughing.'

Grotesque forms that would have made Daumier and Gavarni jealous appeared and disappeared: monstrous creatures performed fantasies decent and indecent. 'If you had been there and seen their performances,' wrote Gautier, 'you would have agreed that the most side-splitting buffoons of our little theatres were fit only to be sculptured on the corners of a tomb.'

Joyous frenzy was now at its height. Loud peals of

laughter had given way to quiet murmurings of ecstasy. Arms stretched out towards fugitive visions. Then one of the club who had not partaken of the *pâté* sat down at a piano, and it seemed to Gautier as if it was he himself who was playing ineffable music. And with the music all the monstrosities slunk away, hiding themselves under chairs or between the folds of curtains.

Again Gautier was alone, and to the noisy gaiety there succeeded an exquisite and indefinable sense of well-being. He felt like a disembodied spirit, he realized the pleasure of angels floating in the heavenly airs. No earthly desires worried him. Romeo had forgotten Juliet. The most beautiful woman in Verona was not worth a moment's thought. Spectres such as those that troubled St Anthony left him undisturbed.

During this reverie Daucus-Carota returned and, squatting before Gautier like a tailor, railed at him with contortions and grimaces. And as he did so Gautier heard a small voice in his ear telling him that the wretched Daucus had robbed him of his head and put in its place, not the head of an ass as Puck had done to Bottom, but the head of an elephant. Gautier struggled to a mirror to find that what he had been told was true. Only by catching Daucus and thumping him against a table was he able to recover his own head.

Then there came a time when, as though a veil had been drawn from across his mind, Gautier realized that the other members of the club were in fact a cabal, intent only on his destruction. With difficulty he rose from his chair and struggled to the door: he reckoned that it took him ten years to cross the room. Pursued by horrors he fought his way down the wide staircase and into the open air. Whereas earlier the courtyard had been sombre and featureless, now its sky-line, with cupolas, towers, and pyramids, was worthy of Rome and Babylon. His surprise was unbounded; never had he suspected that the Île St-Louis contained such monumental magnificences.

And then Daucus appeared before him and, not content with ordering him to return, gripped him and compelled him to climb again those stairs and enter again that great salon from which he had but just escaped. He found it filled with people dressed in black, mourning for Time, Time that had died. Further agonies of mind came upon him, until of a sudden the same musician who had played before sat at the piano a second time and played airs gay and lively. That broke the spell. 'Alleluia, Time is reborn!' cried child-like happy voices.

'Monsieur, your carriage is at the door,' said a man-servant. The hands of the time-piece pointed to eleven o'clock. Gautier had lived an eternity in five hours.

In a parenthesis Gautier states that the hashish of which he partook was the same drug that the 'Old Man of the Mountain' administered to his soldiers on the eve of battle, thus rendering them not only careless of death but eager for it in his cause. This may well be since the name assassin is derived from the Arabian word *hashshashin*, meaning eater of hashish; but in Gautier's words there is also an implication that this was the drug administered to the Old Man's probationary soldiers before they were transferred in a coma to the delectable garden so well described by Marco Polo. Hashish produces hallucinations, the narcotic given to the youths admitted them to reality. If they had experienced the after-effects described by Gautier, few could have wished to experience them a second time, let alone for all eternity.

How different from Gautier's nightmare sequences is Marco's narrative telling how 'in a beautiful valley enclosed between two lofty mountains' the Persian Prince Alo-eddin 'had formed a luxurious garden, stored with every delicious fruit and every shrub that could be procured. Palaces of various sizes and forms were erected in different parts of the grounds, ornamented with works in gold, with paintings, and with furniture of rich silks. By means of small conduits contrived in these buildings, streams of wine, milk, honey, and some of pure water, were seen to flow in every direction. The inhabitants of these palaces were elegant and beautiful damsels, accomplished in the arts of singing, playing upon all sorts of musical instruments, dancing, and especially those of dalliance and amorous allurement. Clothed in rich dresses they were seen continually sporting and amusing themselves in the garden and pavilions, their female guardians being confined within doors and never suffered to appear. The object which the chief had in view in forming a garden of this fascinating kind, was this: that Mahomet having promised to those who should obey his will the enjoyments of Paradise, where every species of sensual gratification should be found in the society of beautiful nymphs, he was desirous of its being understood by his followers that he also was a prophet and the compeer of Mahomet, and had the power of admitting to Paradise such as he should choose to favour. . . . At his court, likewise, this chief entertained a number of youths, from the age of twelve to twenty years, selected from the inhabitants of the surrounding mountains, who showed a disposition for martial exercises, and appeared to possess the quality of daring courage. To them he was in the daily practice of discoursing on the subject of the Paradise announced by the prophet, and of his own power of granting admission; and at certain times he caused draughts of a soporific nature to be administered to ten or a dozen of the youths; and when half dead with sleep he had them conveyed to the several apartments of the palaces in the garden. Upon awakening from the state of lethargy, their senses were struck with all the delightful objects that have been described, and each perceived himself surrounded by lovely damsels, singing, playing, and attracting his regards by the most fascinating caresses, serving him also with delicate viands and exquisite wines; until intoxicated with excess of enjoyment amidst actual rivulets of milk and wine, he believed himself assuredly in Paradise, and felt an unwillingness to relinquish its delights. When four or five days had thus been passed, they were thrown once more into a state of somnolency, and carried out of the garden. Upon their being introduced to his presence, and questioned by him as to where they had been, their

answer was, "In Paradise, through the favour of your highness": and then before the whole court, who listened to them with eager curiosity and astonishment, they gave a circumstantial account of the scenes to which they had been witnesses. The chief thereupon addressing them, said: "We have the assurance of our prophet that he who defends his lord shall inherit Paradise, and if you show yourselves devoted to the obedience of my orders, that happy lot awaits you." Animated to enthusiasm by words of this nature, all deemed themselves happy to receive the commands of their master, and were forward to die in his service.'

From my fourth-floor windows at No. 53 I looked down on to the main channel of the Seine, seeing the barges pass and re-pass, sometimes empty, sometimes heavily loaded with sand or gravel, with timber, coal, cement, or oil. Many moved under their own power, others were towed one, two, three, or even four at a time, by tugs one quarter of their size. I got to know many of those little black tugs by sight, almost all of them named after birds. There were the *Goldfinch,* the *Curlew,* the *Green Wood-pecker,* the *Oriole,* the *Wagtail,* and the *Albatross.* The piercing blasts of their hooters as they came round the point of the island were not so musical as might have been expected from such names, but they soon wove them-selves into the quiet pattern of my days.

Above the houses on the other side of the river rose the spire and towers of Notre-Dame. If there had not been several other churches in the neighbourhood with chiming clocks, I should not have needed a watch. Unfortunately, they all kept different time so that midnight might be announced by thirty or more strokes, a trifle disconcerting at that hour. The lower *quai* under my windows was, like so many others in the city, a setting for both tragedy and romance. At almost any hour of the day pairs of lovers would be seen sitting on the flights of steps that led to the water's edge. At almost any hour of day or night shapeless pieces of humanity would be seen huddled on the cobbles with no more shelter than the poplar leaves high above them. One day as I went to make a drawing on the lower *quai*, I noticed between a tree and the wall an untidy heap of rags. It was only by the crutches lying alongside that I recognized it as a human being, for a loose coat sleeve hid the face. While I looked at him he writhed, slowly, like the last squirm of a cut worm, and I saw his hand under a fold of rag. I had some small coins in my pocket and as I passed I dropped them into the half-open hand. Then, almost frightened by the tortured face that peered up at me, I hurried on. An hour later I passed that place again. This time the old man was sitting with his back to the tree. He looked up as I came near. In that grizzled unwashed face heavy with black unshaven beard were two clear blue eyes, and he gave me the smile of an angel.

Only the next day I had a different experience. As I sat at a corner café of the Rue Jean-du-Bellay, a taxi pulled up in front of me and two men got out. Neither was well dressed but both were alert and active. One of the two paid the driver and then, after a few whispered words, they parted. A little later I had occasion to go down the Rue St-Louis-en-l'Île and, as I did so, I saw ahead of me a street singer with hat in hand, limping badly. He was the one who had paid for the taxi. Charitable folk were coming out of doors to drop money into his hat.

At the far end of this street is the Hôtel Lambert where Voltaire lived for four years with Madame du Châtelet. Carlyle speaks of the lady as 'that scientific and too-fascinating shrew,' who 'speculated in mathematics and metaphysics; but was an adept also in far, very far different acquirements.' Their life together, he says, was a matter of 'short sun-gleams, with long, tropical tornadoes; touches of guitar-music, soon followed by Lisbon earthquakes.'

If my studio had all the amenities that I could wish for during the day, it did not lack interest at night. No sooner had I switched off the bedside lamp than the whole ceiling was suffused with quivering light reflected from the river. Direct light came upwards also from the street lamps and cast great luminous blazons through the open windows. These shone again at opposing angles in the large mirror between the windows. When a tourist steamer passed with roving searchlights, it was as if a silver net had caught the room and sent it wheeling—a merry-go-round of stars and meteors. On the other side of the river the flood-lit towers of Notre-Dame shone white against a glow from unseen neon lamps, and the sky, dense as velvet, was varied as velvet that is brushed.

The sounds, too, would alter. As in a tropical forest at night the great creatures cease to growl, birds cease to sing, monkeys stop their chattering, and only the multitudinous insects make their clamour, so after midnight would harsh sounds die down, and I would hear little but the rhythmic pulse of distant traffic.

CHAPTER TWENTY-ONE

THE LAST kind of an affair in which I had expected to become embroiled in Paris was the home life of a pair of pigeons. It was only a few days after I had settled in to the studio that I noticed two of these birds, with apparently mutual interests, among the poplars that overhung the river. Next morning I realized that they had begun to build, and had chosen a fork of a tree that could scarcely have been closer to my windows. How was my observation of this romance going to fit in with the visits of Nicole, the model? I wondered. My friend Willy Moren had promised to bring her along that afternoon. She was blonde, and he wanted to paint her as a foreground to the sunlit poplar-trees. I need not have worried: Nicole was only free to pose in the afternoons and, as I soon discovered, the pigeons only did their building in the mornings. As I came to know them better it surprised me how ordered was their way of life. Romance in the evening, but in the morning cold matter-of-fact work. Where they roosted, or if they roosted beside each other during the time of building, I do not know; they neither left together in the evenings nor returned together in the mornings.

In their daily routine the hen was always the first to appear, usually some half-hour after dawn. The cock would arrive a little later. There was no greeting that I could see: he just assured himself that she was on the nest and then went off to find the first stick of the day. Bringing it back, he would climb up behind her and, sometimes treading on her back as though she were part of the nest, he would lean over and lay the twig before her. Then as she picked it up, put it where she thought fit, and pressed down with her body to mould it into place, he would glide in the direction of the gardens of Notre-Dame to find another.

Everything about Nicole was *petite* except her brown eyes; they were enormous. She wished that her nose wasn't quite so long, but the length of her legs pleased her. She also liked the dimples low down on her back, and none other than Domergue had told her that her hips were good. Willy suggested that she should lean against the rail of my window and look out across the river; her body would then be suffused in the same golden light as the trees. But Nicole had doubts about the screening power of the poplars. There were gaps between the branches, she said, and there were many windows just across the water. So we hung a yellow cotton shirt of mine on the rail, and she leaned on that. The sun shone through the garment and she became the centre of a halo.

Willy at one side of the studio worked on an upright canvas, I at the other side on a horizontal panel. Did I mind the scraping sound of the coarse brush? he asked, as he scrubbed in the first tones. His wife couldn't bear it. I said that provided he didn't crunch apples or cranch sweets I could bear anything. Nicole said that what made her wince was the tearing of silk or cotton. It was as if her own insides were being torn.

Willy thought that such idiosyncrasies, common to so many people, must refer back to prenatal experiences. They might even be racial in their origin. I said that someone had defined imagination as concentrated race experience. Might not these irritant noises have some connection with primitive fears—the cracking of twigs that meant danger, the tearing of flesh, the crunching of bones?

We painted for about an hour and then rested. Willy's canvas was a blaze of prismatic colour: I could hardly make out where the girl was meant to be. He said he would work the form into the colour later. My panel was a complete contrast: I had searched for the forms and pattern in monochrome: it was the colour that I would add later. The wind was rising and from time to time small clouds hid the sun. Nicole began to shiver, but we told her that *she* must suffer for *our* art. She did so for another half-hour and then the sun really did disappear.

It was after seven o'clock that same evening when, looking upwards from my window, I saw the two pigeons on another branch. Their crops were full and they looked double the size of their morning selves. Such billings and such carryings-on as followed I never did see. Under the feathers of their necks and throats each would in turn caress the other. Stretching up their heads they would stroke bill against bill. They were scarce twenty feet above me and I could see the pulsations in their breasts. Then they mated. After only a moment's pause the endearments began again—back of the neck, under the eyes, especially under the feathers of the throat. Then they mated a second time. Within another few minutes the cycle had been completed for the third time. Then together they floated down to a lower branch and after contemplating their work of the morning flew away, first one and then the other. By now Notre-Dame was striking nine o'clock and the colour had faded from the sky. Like the birds, I went to bed.

At 4.20 next morning sparrows were chirping and swifts were in the air, but there was no sign of the pigeons until 4.30 when the hen appeared. She sat on a lower bough, preening occasionally, and did not make her way up to the incipient nest until near five o'clock. At 5.15 the cock arrived, threw a casual look at his mate, and flew away again. He came back a quarter of an hour later and this time perched beside her and, though he carried nothing, made bowing gestures as if of putting down sticks. Then he flew away once more. Before his first arrival the hen had been quiet, almost motionless, but now, stimulated by his appearance, she began to move about on the nest, moulding it with her breast. Within a few minutes the cock returned and this time he carried a twig. The morning's work had begun. They continued with zeal till towards midday; during the afternoon they disappeared; in the late evening they came again to the upper branch. It was the same routine as on the day before—a good programme, I thought; work in the morning, picnic in the afternoon, love in the evening, and then to sleep.

Next morning on my side of the windows work began on a still life: bananas and tomatoes in a green bowl on a table covered with a pale blue cloth. A book beside the bowl accented the rectangle of the table, the curves of the bananas were pleasant variants of the circular pottery rim, while the red of the tomatoes and of a cloak that hung behind them, though mildly discordant among themselves, gave emphasis to the gentle yellows, greens, and blue.

The cock was now doing much of his collecting from some dead upper branches on a neighbouring tree and many of the sticks that he was bringing to the nest were lighter than those he had brought for the foundations. When making his way along a thin and bending twig to snap at one still thinner, he would move sideways, balancing himself with half-open wings. He always tweaked the smaller twig backwards so that it broke off at the joint.

Some though bare had life in them and would not break, others came away easily. His return to the nest was always the same, perching first on the sloping trunk of the tree some eight or ten feet below the nest and then walking slowly upwards. When as happened sometimes he had difficulty in manœuvring an extra long twig through the foliage that surrounded the nest, the hen would stretch out her neck and help him. His departure, also, was always the same. A few steps to a small branch that arched above the nest, and from there a gentle glide.

Two mornings later activity at the nest had slowed down. Though the hen was there the cock put in few appearances, and when he did arrive it was without material for the nest. But about two o'clock in the afternoon there was a break in the routine. As the cock walked slowly up the bough the hen rose to greet him. Then together they looked into the nest and began to bow, raising and lowering their heads a number of times in quick succession. After that the hen flew away and for the first time the cock settled down in her place. I felt sure that an egg had been laid. For the next seventeen days it was turn and turn about on the nest, the cock sitting during the day and the hen at night.

CHAPTER TWENTY-TWO

ONE MORNING soon after this event, Nicole rang me up to say that Willy was out of Paris but that she was free to sit that afternoon if I wished. So at about four o'clock she came along and we worked for an hour. She talked rather a lot, but she explained that she thought it a good thing that we should *nous mettre en rapport*. She told me that on no account would she exhibit herself at a cabaret or music-hall. It was quite a different thing to pose for artists: artists were pure. I was glad to hear that. At about five o'clock I said that I must stop awhile to watch for the return of the hen pigeon. The cock had been taking over brooding each morning within a few minutes of half past nine, but the hen was not so consistent in her times of arrival. I suggested to Nicole that she should amuse herself as she pleased while I sat at the window and waited. As I took up my binoculars she began to potter around, picking up books and putting them down again, turning over loose drawings, glancing at canvases that leaned against the wall. Then, soon after I sat down, there was silence and I forgot that she was there.

The pigeon came back at 5.35, and after I had made a note of the time I got up to continue work. There before me was Nicole standing at the easel with my palette

on her thumb, and a corner of the studio sketched on a panel.

'C'est joli?' she asked.

'Très joli,' I said.

No, she had never painted before, she said—it was the first time in her life that she had even held a palette. She continued dabbing while she spoke, and I could see from the way she stood close up to the easel 'painting with her nose,' and the way she held her brush as a child holds a pen, close up to the nib, that what she said was true. Did I wish then to get on with my painting? she asked. I said,

'No, stay as you are. You are a better subject at the easel than at the window.'

It was a hot afternoon and she hadn't bothered to put on clothes while resting; apart from the palette on her thumb, her only dress was a thin gold necklace. The flowing contours of her limbs were a nice opposition to the rigid lines of the easel. We continued work while the light lasted, she with colours, I in black and white.

'Did you enjoy yourself?' I asked, as she put down the brushes.

'It was the nicest pose of my life!' she said.

Each day afterwards that she sat for me I stopped work in time to give her half an hour with my palette, and each time she did a charming if naïve sketch. Books, bottles, tea-cups, dropped into pleasant arrangements from her hands as flowers do from green fingers. I inquired one day if she had many sittings with other artists. Oh yes, she said, she had been going every morning to a sculptor to pose as the Blessed Virgin. He was doing a big statue for somewhere in Rome. It was nearly finished. I asked if I could see it and she said certainly, she could arrange that quite easily.

So a few days later she took me to the studio. The sculptor was out when we arrived but the door was open and two of his assistants were there at work. They were building a plaster mould around the feet of a clay figure— a naked girl on tiptoe with a star above her forehead.

'You think it is like me?' asked Nicole.

'Very like *you*,' I said, 'but I thought it was to be the Blessed Virgin?'

'The Assumption,' said one of the assistants. 'She is just leaving the earth.'

This was a bit surprising.

Just then the sculptor came in. 'Yes,' he said, 'the Assumption. It is for the Vatican.'

This was even more surprising.

'I like to get the figure into plaster first,' he said. 'Then I can manipulate the draperies.' He pointed to a quantity of cotton material that lay on the floor. "My wife makes the garments,' he went on. 'Then I dip them into the liquid plaster and I mould them on to the body. They set very quickly; one can put one garment on top of another. It is the only way to be accurate. When they are all set and hard it is easy for my masons to copy in stone.'

I had forgotten that such methods still existed. I knew that in painting and engraving it is often necessary to make sketches of the figures that underlie the draperies— only by absolute knowledge of the action of the body can the folds of the garments be made to emphasize that action; but I had come to think of sculpture in stone as a direct carving of a clear vision, a release of the figure imprisoned within the stone. Studies would, of course, have been made, perhaps hundreds of them, but only to clarify that vision in the artist's mind before he began the setting free.

Perhaps in this I have grown out of date; fashionable forms of sculpture change almost as quickly as fashionable forms in human femininity—one day curves, the next straight lines. It is only a few years since mass was what mattered in sculpture; 'let the figure be of the medium,' it was said; 'take away the least possible amount of the stone or wood, solidity and bulk are among the essentials.' To-day the approach is from the other extreme: take thin wire and add as little as possible to it, seems to be the slogan. The wire is used almost as a pen line, to express literary ideas, and plastic form is left in the clay bin.

The naked line has also found its way to pictorial design, and subjects that might better have been expressed with the beauty of an etched line are sprawled over large areas of canvas and lack almost all the pleasing qualities of pigment. For me every inch of a painting should have intrinsic interest, should glow as a precious stone. This may be a narrow view, but then, as Wilde said, only an auctioneer can admire all schools of Art.

Nicole continued to sit for me, and one afternoon I managed to achieve something of the calligraphic quality that I had been seeking. The light had changed and there was but an hour to go. 'Take an easy pose on the divan,' I said.

She lay down with her back towards me and I suspect went to sleep. The pose was simple and I let the brushes wander, moulding the forms of flesh and cushions in colours that seemed already mixed. Nothing of a pose, nothing of a painting—but 'loose' at last!

Next time Nicole came to sit she was pale and tired.

She couldn't stop yawning. It was the fault of her fiancé, she said. He had gone with others to see a negro dancer at the Alhambra and hadn't taken her. It was the first time in two years that he had done such a thing. He was so cross with her when she was cross with him that he had taken her by the arms and shaken her: the two big bruises on each arm were where he had gripped her. She didn't want ever to see him again.

'So all is over between you?' I asked.

'Oh no,' she said. 'I love him too much.'

The restaurants on the Île St-Louis were not of the modest excellence that I had expected; but here and there in the neighbourhood I found small places that suited my ambition. At one of them on the eastern extremity of the Île de la Cité, I became friendly with a waiter whose home was in the Savoie. His name was Pignaz Philibert, and he spoke in such a strong patois that few people could understand him. But his exuberance of spirits carried him through. His infectious gaiety was such that inevitably I found myself in conversation with those at neighbouring tables. He made up his mind that I was just the man to spend a holiday with him in his mountains, and he was so full of the project that I hadn't the heart to tell him that high mountains made me ill. He showed me photos of his farm 3,000 feet up, under overhanging rocks whose fall seemed imminent. Last winter the house had been buried for a week under an avalanche. Each day that he came to my table it was with another inducement

to visit him. We would go chamois hunting together. It
was wonderful to hear the shot echoing in the mountains
and to carry home the dead animal. Oh yes, certainly, it
meant climbing, but I would soon get used to that. And
think of the evenings around the big wood fire with plenty
of *vin rouge* at fifty francs the litre! If the weather was
cold we could sleep with the cattle. The shepherds did
that regularly in winter. They kept very big dogs, he said.
He had just had a letter saying that one of them had killed
one of his best sheep, a black ewe worth ten thousand
francs. It had torn its throat open. It would be as well
to carry a strong stick if I went out alone. Last year one
of the dogs had killed a cow and eaten much of its belly.
As a further attraction he showed me a photograph of
some vipers on a rock. 'There are very many of them,'
he said.

'Dangerous?' I suggested.

'Leur venin est mortel' he said.

Before he left Paris he lent me a book which told of
life in the Savoie. A week after he had departed I received a postcard. 'Here fine weather. One eats well,
drinks much. Good brandy, good wine. Beautiful country. I count on you. I have prepared your bed. You
know my address. I will meet you at the station—with the
fire brigade if you wish. Come with heavy boots for the
hunting. Pignaz.'

It was a picture postcard, and the picture had for sub-
title, 'An interior where the question of heating does not
arise.' It showed under a vaulted roof, on the left, a num-

ber of cattle in their stalls; on the right, separated from the creatures by no more than a low wooden partition, a comfortable looking wooden bed with blue and white striped coverlet and a blue and crimson pillow. Above the bed hung a crucifix and some religious pictures.

The book which Pignaz had lent me showed many of these habitations shared equally by the family and their creatures: cattle, sheep, goats, mule, and pig. Usually a gutter running from end to end of the abode divided the human inhabitants from the animals, and usually the pig pen was in the furthest corner. The book showed too the precipices and rugged escarpments, the crevasses and ravines, among which I was expected to skip in pursuit of chamois.

I wrote to Pignaz and said that I must postpone my visit till I had grown younger.

CHAPTER TWENTY-THREE

I HAD NOT been in the studio a fortnight before I found myself in the beginnings of a decline. At first I thought it might be some delayed result of all the hill climbing I had done in Italy and that I would soon recover; but no, the symptoms grew more and more pronounced. It wasn't that I was feeling ill, it was just that my waist line was shrinking. I noticed it when my trousers had grown so loose that I had to move the buttons of the belt. Twice in one week I moved them more than an inch, and yet by the end of the following week another alteration was necessary. It was worrying because it wasn't as if I'd been starving myself. I could only suppose that I wasn't making good use of my food. And then one night I went out to dinner with some friends and our hostess provided a meal that was as nourishing as it was filling. This will put me right surely, I thought. It did. When I rose from my arm-chair to say good-bye, my trousers nearly fell off! This time the elastic had gone completely. It wasn't me that had been perishing. Relieved of all anxiety, I walked home gaily, a hand in either trouser pocket.

Among the many culinary perfections to be found in Paris bread ranks high. Those truncheons of crisp brown crust, still warm from the baker's oven, are a twice-daily delight. But their peak of perfection is short-lived. From crispness through toughness to hardness they move with disheartening speed. It was a problem how to preserve some of that ephemeral beauty even for a few hours. Then one day I noticed that whenever I bought a bottle of anything important it was wrapped in tissue-paper. Would not a few sheets of that keep the air from the bread and so preserve its crispness? It did, and so by occasional visits to *La Vendangeuse* I managed to keep my bread fresh.

At one small restaurant on the north side of the river I found a perfect cuisine, and for a time I was a 'regular' for dinner with my own napkin kept for me from day to day. Before sitting down I would have an aperitif with the *patron* at his zinc-topped bar just inside the door, and while so doing Madame or her daughter would bring me the menu written in chalk on a slate. When my orders were ready I had only to step back two paces to my table and continue from there whatever discussion was in progress. One evening it concerned the dead fish in the river —many thousands of them floating belly upwards. For two days they had been coming down. Some factory upstream had discharged chlorine into the water. They did the same thing last year, just at the same time, at the beginning of the holidays, spoiling all sport. Something should be done about it. Another day the talk was of a man who had committed suicide that afternoon. He certainly had made sure of the result, tying a cord around his neck to the bridge before he jumped. Though the cord had broken he must have been unconscious when he hit the river. But his face was peaceful when they dragged him out—almost as if he were smiling.

Other regulars would drop in for a drink or a game of dominoes. Among them was a show girl from a nearby theatre who came regularly each evening for one drink only, *un Ricard*, before going on to her work.

The *patron* introduced me, suggesting to her jokingly that she should pose for me. 'I have but one ambition of artists,' she said, 'that some day one of them will ask to paint me fully dressed.'

The pity about that restaurant was that too often Madame would drink just a little too much too early. 'What, already?' her husband would say to her sadly. On those occasions she would come to my table and ask me to marry her. *Tournedos, châteaubriants,* or even *rognons en brochettes* do not digest well with proposals of marriage, and I was forced to go elsewhere.

My windows looked across the river to the Quai aux Fleurs, where on six days a week a flower market is held. On the seventh day, Sunday, the flowers disappear, and in their stead thousands of tiny birds are offered for sale. It is hard to say which are the brighter, the colours of the petals or the colours of the feathers. Cardinals with crimson heads from Brazil; flame-breasted flutists from Karachi; yellow serins from Mozambique; golden sparrows from Arabia; Bengalis, blue, silver, and coral, sociable little birds that only thrive when many are together.

The thought of what some of these small creatures may

have suffered since they were first trapped or netted, their days of journeying overland carried in boxes on the heads of porters and their subsequent sea voyage in overcrowded cages, is not a pleasant one; but in fact the great majority appear to have been bred in France and only a few seem discontented with their lot. Every sort of bird food is offered for sale from maize and peanuts to the tiny millet and carnation seeds. One can get ants' eggs, assortments of maggots, cuttle-fish bones, and bunches of green plantain, chick-weed, or groundsel. I noticed small bundles of fresh grass. 'Those are for the dogs and cats,' I was told, and the old woman at the stall added: 'In Paris one can buy anything.'

She sold also small nests woven of reeds, and bunches of moss and fibre with which the birds might line them.

'Do they breed easily here, these tropicals?' I asked her.

'If you love them and make them love you—yes,' she said.

Such love is shown in the narrative of Madame Feuillée-Billot, assistant secretary-general of the French league for the protection of birds, when she tells of the loss of one of her favourites. 'It was a *ministre* from Central America, a superb bird in whose plumage was blended peacock blue, cobalt, and ultramarine. It had just settled down in the special quarters that I had prepared for it when the war broke out. Then from all sides they brought me birds whose owners had rejoined their regiments. I agreed to look after several hundreds of the more delicate exotic species in a room hurriedly prepared for them, but by a misunderstanding they brought me two thousand. It was enough to make me lose my head, and I had the unfortunate idea of letting my own birds, with whom I was so intimate, mix with all these stranger refugees. When my *ministre* saw himself in the middle of such a crowd he was overcome with panic. Never shall I forget the look of despair with which he asked to be taken from that room. At the time I did not fully understand this, but next day, looking for him everywhere, I found at last the little sapphire body behind the radiator where he had gone to hide himself and die.'

On the ground in front of the old woman's stall were sacks with special seed mixtures for canaries, for parakeets, for goldfinches, and for many other birds. I bought a litre of the mixture for pigeons. My couple would be wanting a bit of maize to keep them warm for the hatching, I thought. Hitherto I had only been putting bread for them on my window-sill.

As time went on Monsieur and Madame, as I had come to call them, became regular visitors. Morning and evening, as each was relieved at the nest it would come and perch on the window-ledge and there await my offering of corn. They always moved with great dignity, no unseemly hurry, and they picked the grains as epicures, quite unlike a pair of blue rocks who also came to the windows and behaved like hooligans, jostling each other and making such a disturbance with their wings that half the grain was blown on to the street below.

On the seventeenth morning after hatching had begun,

the hen seemed reluctant to leave the nest, staying there quite awhile after the cock had returned. That evening she came back an hour earlier than usual and was restless, sitting, it seemed to me, rather high on the nest and constantly probing under her breast with her bill. Next morning there was no doubt of what had happened. I could see her regurgitating food to at least one youngster. She did so at 6.30, at 7, and again at 7.40 and 8.15. Then at 9.30 she extracted from under her feathers an empty shell which she carried away in her bill and dropped at a safe non-revealing distance from the nest. She was away hardly more than a minute, but the chicks received no more nourishment till some time after the cock's appearance at 10.10. As in his usual way he walked slowly up the sloping branch towards the nest, the hen greeted him with much bowing of the head, similar to their mutual gestures after the laying of the first egg. He showed no surprise at this, but as she seemed reluctant to leave he almost shouldered her from the edge of the nest and took his place inside. I did not wait to see him feed his offspring, for it was now half past ten and I myself had been brooding for more than four hours. Feeling the need of a couple of eggs under my own plumage, I retired to the kitchen.

There were times when, sitting in my arm-chair watching the behaviour of those birds for hours at a time, I felt not unlike old père Toine in Maupassant's story who, because he was stout and had become bedridden, was compelled by his shrew of a wife to brood a clutch of eggs, five on either side of him. My chair did not fit me very well and without sitting on them I could easily have tucked in a dozen behind me where they would have been cosy and warm. I wondered whether, when they hatched, I would have felt the same maternal emotions as did père Toine, who tenderly kissed the last little one that arrived and wished to keep it with him in his bed.

The story of Toine may be doubted by some, but eggs have their own peculiar means of withstanding pressure. It is not so long since, when visiting a neighbour, I found after half an hour in an arm-chair that I had been sitting on an egg laid there by the family hen just before my arrival. There wasn't even a crack in the shell.

CHAPTER TWENTY-FOUR

THOUGH I AM a lover of solitude I agree with Robinson Crusoe when, in his *Serious Reflections*, he writes: 'I can affirm that I enjoy much more solitude in the middle of the greatest collection of mankind in the world, I mean, at London, while I am writting this, than ever I could say I enjoyed in eight and twenty years' confinement to a desolate island.'

Without casting one grain of coral dust at the 'desert' islands on which I have spent idyllic days and nights, I must admit that it was this Defoe form of solitude that I found and enjoyed on the Île St-Louis. There in the heart of Paris, with the river flowing past on either side, I was as isolated as a lake dweller, yet within easy reach of any sophistication that might momentarily become needful to my soul.

It was one evening after two days alone with the pigeons that I slipped across the footbridge and made my way through the ill-lit Rue du Cloître-Notre-Dame, across the *parvis* of the cathedral, and along the Quai des Orfèvres (goldsmiths) to the little triangular chestnut-shaded Place Dauphine. There I hoped to dine Chez Paul. But it was late when I arrived and not only was every table occupied but every available extra table had already been brought up from the cellar and set upon the pavement. I was about to move on when the *patron* came to tell me that in five minutes, perhaps ten at the most, there would be a table free. Then, after I had agreed, he added that there were two other clients who had just come in by the door from the *quai,* one of them an Englishman: perhaps I would not mind sharing my table with them. So I sat on one of the benches under the trees in the Place to await my call.

As things turned out I did not have long to wait, just time enough to think on Henri IV who had himself designed the Place and called it after his son the Dauphin, afterwards Louis XIII. Henri had visualized it as a centre of commerce, but it did not develop as he had hoped. Instead, during the eighteenth century it became an exhibition ground for artists, and there on canvas screens, as we see to-day in Montparnasse on Sundays, young painters now famous—Boucher, Nattier, Chardin, and others—first showed their work to the public.

Henri, 'the father of his people,' rides in bronze splendour almost at the head of the Place: some use the phrase 'the father of many of his people,' for history has handed down the names of fifty-six of his mistresses and, as André Maurois has remarked in this connection, Clio, the Muse of History, does not know all. It was Henri, the Protestant king of a Catholic people, who in a time of bitter intolerance said: 'Those who follow their consciences are of my religion, and my religion is that of all those who are brave and honest men.' It was he also who wished that even for the poorest of his subjects there should be a chicken in the pot every Sunday.

Just when my thoughts were on the chicken, I was summoned indoors and shown to a table. An enormously stout man with a high domed almost bald head was already there, and sitting opposite to him a slight intense-looking woman with a heavy truss of golden hair standing out from the back of her head. As I sat down beside her, for there was little space on the other side, the waiter brought three brandies and put them on the table. Without a word the stout gentleman tipped them into a large glass, added a few drops from the siphon and drank the lot. Beckoning to the waiter he said: 'Remettez ça!'

The waiter obeyed the order and the stout gentleman repeated the operation. Then with a gentle smile he looked across the table. 'You must excuse me,' he said, 'but I am just coming to the surface.' He then began to talk, very softly in measured phrases, and I soon learned that he was a poet—not many works done but many great works undone, as Browning might have said. His companion called him Mark. He introduced her as his wife Maria and addressed her as Ria. She, it seemed, had once been a mannequin but was now a dancer. Her former work had taught her the symbolic value of draperies, she told me. It was with simple movements allied to simple draperies that she was hoping to express some of the elemental ferments of life.

Mark was English but lived in France; his wife was French but had spent some years in England during the war. We spoke a mixture of French and English, some-

times one, sometimes the other. I liked them both—he
so bulky, dreamy and gentle, she eager and sensitive.

When the menus were brought, I noticed a dish called
Côtelettes de veau en papillotes. 'That is something new
to me,' I said.

'Then you must try it here—it is a speciality of the
house,' said Maria. 'Many people think it is the best way
of cooking veal, with herbs and mushrooms and onions.
But it is the method of cooking that is the secret. Certainly it is one of the oldest and most famous of French
recipes.'

After the waiter had taken our orders and Mark had
reached the surface by a third libation, he said to me:
'You travel wisely.'

As I did not immediately appreciate his inference, he
continued: 'It is one of the perquisites of travel that it
keeps the palette flexible—perhaps perceptive is a better
word. Our sense of taste is constantly stimulated: we are
compelled to consider and pronounce upon new flavors—
that is, of course, if we are not of those who know what
they like. To know what one likes in food and to be
satisfied with it is as paralysing to the digestion as to know
what one likes in art is deadening to aesthetic develop-
ment.'

'It is always difficult to break from inside a sphere,' said
Maria. 'Most people live in armour whose inner surface
is so polished that it reflects only their own thoughts, and
the outside is so polished that it deflects other people's
ideas.'

'The tendency in life,' said Mark, 'is to gather the fibres of our own experience into such a network around us that they become a cocoon from which escape is impossible.'

At this juncture our veal arrived, each piece still wrapped in the dark paper in which it had been cooked. Deservedly we gave the dish our full attention.

To go with the coffee Mark ordered brandies for all three of us. 'I suffer from a complaint,' he said, 'that needs brandy before and after dinner. I do not drink during the day but in the evening I have a tendency to become drowsy—I think it is due to my weight.' I admitted to an occasional drowsiness myself.

'I wonder,' said Ria, as we rose to go, 'if you would come back with us to our studio? I am dancing to-night and I should like an audience. There is an arm-chair in which you can go to sleep if you wish. Mark will certainly go to sleep in his. But he will write a beautiful poem afterwards; he says he watches me through his closed lids.'

Their studio was only a short distance away, in a side street off the Quai du Louvre on the north side of the river. It was on the fourth floor; the stairs were steep and there was no lift. 'It is these steps that keep my weight down,' panted Mark; Ria was already out of sight above us.

The studio was long and narrow with a kitchen and a bedroom opening from one side. At the far end in an alcove was a small curtained stage. Ria went into the bedroom to change her dress and Mark began to grind coffee in the kitchen. While I was waiting the door-bell rang and I let in a man with a short red beard carrying a musical instrument case, and a woman whose dark hair was cut into crisp curls all over her head. Ria hurried from the bedroom to greet them. She was now wearing a duffel coat over what appeared to be a white silk night-dress. She introduced them as Jules and Madeleine Armand, he a photographer, she a musician. Then she led Madeleine to the bedroom, leaving me to talk to Jules.

Mark called from the kitchen that he was having trouble with the coffee grinder; a cog had come loose, but he would be along in a moment. He handed Jules a bottle of Delamain brandy—one could not want a better—and some glasses. I inferred that he did not wish us to become drowsy.

'You know,' said Jules, 'that Jacques Delamain was a writer as well as a distiller?'

'I know that he was a great lover of nature,' I said, 'and I have his book in English, *Why Birds Sing*. It doesn't tell you why they sing but it is a delightful book.'

Ria and Madeleine joined us, Ria having exchanged the duffel coat for a brocaded house robe. Mark appeared with the coffee.

'Jules specializes in the photography of hats, pipes, and dogs,' he said.

At this the red bristles on Jules's chin bid fair to stand on end. 'I specialize in the *refusal* to have such things in my portraits,' he said. 'If a man has so little character in his head that he needs to hide one half of it with a hat, or if his face is so empty that he needs a pipe to fill it, or if a woman needs a dog——' He did not finish the sentence; his wife had taken a Tyrolean zither from its case and begun to tune it. I got the impression that she had heard these remarks more than once before.

Coffee and local gossip followed. The current joke in one of the art schools was that the professor of sculpture had told a student that when carving elm wood he should always choose a female tree. The wood is kinder and less knotted than in the male, he said, and the student—a boy from Provence—had answered: 'But in the *country* elm-trees have not different sexes—the flower is both male and female.'

Then they asked me if I had met Bella—Bella the beachcomber. How had I escaped? My day would come!

'Watch your shirt,' said Jules. 'She's had mine already, a purple one that Madeleine dyed for me. Said she had to have it—it expressed her ego. Up at the Deux Magots the other night she made me take it off and give it to her.'

'Watch for leopard-skin trousers,' said Madeleine. 'They also express her ego.'

'Who and what is she?' I asked.

'A girl from across the Atlantic, scrounging her way around the world—thinks it's clever. Makes jewellery out of bottle tops.'

'Do they also express her ego?' I asked.

'Her ego is all-embracing,' said Ria with, I thought, a touch of malice.

Now it was time for the business of the evening. Ria left us to change her dress once more. Mark switched lights on and off. Madeleine with her zither moved nearer the stage; Jules shifted chairs to face the stage. I mused quietly on the works of Jacques Delamain.

At last all was ready. Madeleine struck some notes on the zither, and the curtains were drawn apart to reveal Ria crouched low and heavily shrouded in folds of russet linen. The music began again, a slow, primitive rhythm as of forest drums, repeat and repeat with but slight variations. Then to the same measure two hands emerged from the drapery, opening and closing with palms upward as if in supplication. Following a sudden plucking of deep chords, there was a moment's silence, and then came a staccato high-pitched chant increasing in speed and volume. With the change in tempo the figure began to rise, the hands, together and pointed upwards, emerging as the tip of a growing shoot from its enveloping sheath. Inch by inch it stretched upwards and as slowly the drapery fell away until with Ria on tiptoe it lay like earth about her feet. She was wearing what I had taken to be a night-dress, a closely fitting ivory white garment, indicative yet non-revealing as on Egyptian figurines. Her truss of hair had been loosened and let fall over her shoulders so that her features were framed in, as it were, a wealth of golden petals. Now her hands came down close to her sides and her head with closed eyes was thrown back:

above the gentle modulations of her body her face seemed like a flower lifted to the sun. The music stopped, the dance was over. The rain had fallen and earth had brought forth.

Various phases of the dance and its accompaniment were reviewed. Might not the change of metaphor be too abrupt from the sharp chords that symbolized an answer to supplication to the pattering notes that implied the falling of rain? The one was an abstraction, the other realistic.

Then Maria got up to explore the possibilities of a sun dance. She took from the wall a large circular disk with a gold filigree rim. This was the sun. She would represent earth. Holding it low on the left of the stage, the eastern side, she would make it rise and describe an orbit above her head until it dropped again and set in the west. By the movements and gestures of her body she had to express the calm of dawn, the exultancy of noon, and then again the quiet of evening. Just when she was agreeing upon the music with Madeleine the lights fused. There followed black darkness but for the flickers of two cigarette lighters, one of which faded out quickly from want of spirit. There was no fuse wire in the house: Ria explained that only that morning a sculptor friend had borrowed it for a *mobile* that he was making. By the light of a match she found a stump of candle and stood it on an ash-tray. Mark emptied the last of the brandy into our glasses and stuck the candle into the neck of the bottle.

As the wick swallowed its last gouts of molten wax, I followed Jules and Madeleine to the door.

CHAPTER TWENTY-FIVE

A SUDDEN blanket of heat smothered the city. It was tangible: at every corner that one turned it seemed more dense. The swimming-pools along the Seine were crowded, and as if the Prefect of Police, unlike the weather bureau, had had foreknowledge of the high temperatures there appeared beside the entrance of each pool the following notice:

In 1954 decency for men was measured in centimetres. As for women, what they wore wouldn't have made sails for toy yachts. How silly these jibs and stern sails are, revealing more than concealing; all the more so when the rigging of a cutter is carried on a schooner.

But I think I have more than once before expressed myself on the subject of swim-suits, so for the nonce let us talk of the joys of pigments. Could anything be more lovely than zinc white as it is squidged from the tube on to a palette, radiating light and enhancing all with which it is commingled. Reds of the madder root and blues of the cobalt rock, golds and greens of cadmium and chrome, all wake and sing when touched by that white wand. Of course, there are petty squabbles on the palette as in all large families. Cadmium yellow must not touch vermilion lest there be black warfare; emerald green, brilliant in itself, destroys all others. But brothers that quarrel at the table are allied in the field. The artist if a tactful parent gives to all his boys and girls their chance to shine.

And after pigments, among the sensuous delights of painting, must come the holding of a well-made brush, its handle perfectly tapered and balanced, its faintly curving bristles seeming to grow into the filbert shape, the long fat, the long flat, or any other symmetry that the predilections of an artist may demand.

'Yes,' said Mr Mares who for nearly 150 years (with the help of his father and grandfather) has been making for James Newman of London what I think are the loveliest brushes in the world. 'Yes,' he said, 'you can only do it by hand, every brush by hand.' As he spoke he took a pinch of bristles and laid them in his left palm. Then with his right hand he began to tap that palm. 'Look,' he said. 'You can see the bristles turning, their curves are fitting naturally into each other. Now it is only a matter of rolling them inwards. Well, yes,' he admitted, 'it does take a few years to learn.'

I told him that only the day before I had been to the

Earl's Court cattle show, and had been admiring the white, shining bristles of the prize pigs, so *soignés* for the occasion.

'The best bristles come from France,' he said, showing me two packets, one labelled *Beau Blanc* and the other *Fine Droit*. 'Both have a good point but the *Beau Blanc* is a bit stiffer.' Then he added: 'They don't kill the animal and take the lot at once over there: they pluck a few of the best bristles each year.'

He showed me also sables—from the tail of the animal, better in winter than in summer; and weasels, the same colour but slightly coarser; and squirrels for water-colour skies, and badgers and ox for many purposes from sign writing to French polishing. But it was the hogs, that lift and mix and spread the oil colours so firmly yet so gently on the canvas, that held my wonder and affection.

I don't want to drag fat cattle into my studio in Paris, but I can't forbear to say a few words about Hilda, 'the supreme champion animal' of that show, an Aberdeen Angus heifer. To what did she attribute her success, her bulk, her beauty? Let me whisper the answer: she attributed all to nothing else than whisky by-products. The man who cared for her upbringing was not only the foreman of her farm but also the foreman of a large distillery, and he knew what the growing girl needed.

And now, talking of growing girls and studios, though unconnected with even the little lambs at the cattle show, I am reminded of a happy episode that once came my way. It was many years ago, soon after I had first settled in

London and was beginning my career as an engraver, that I was invited to dine by a party of twelve American girls who, with their tutor-chaperone, were touring Europe. In the various cities which they visited, it was part of their curriculum to entertain each evening some artist, poet, or other exponent of uplift, who would discourse to them on the niceties of his trade. And for this particular occasion they had chosen me. Someone had told them that I was busy in the revival of wood-engraving, and they wanted to know the difference, if any, between a woodcut and a wood-carving.

The dinner was a success—the girls were as charming as they were good-looking and I had no difficulty in talking. After our meal we moved to their private sitting-room, and whilst I continued my chatter one of them, deeply interested, asked where it would be possible to see some of my work. That was what I had been hoping for, what I had indeed prepared for.

'It's a strange chance,' I said, 'but I happen to have collected some prints from a gallery this afternoon and I've left them in the cloak-room.'

But that was fine! Would I not fetch them?

Why, of course! The collection that I then produced contained two engravings of nude girls stepping into pools. There were also houses under snow in Dublin, and houses under sunshine in Malta, and some spotted cows in County Cork; but the girls liked the nudes best. Yes, the general opinion was that such subjects were my line. I should certainly do more of them, they said. Then one of them asked why I had not already done more, and I, forgetting that for the moment I was a 'lion,' answered that I couldn't afford models.

'You can't afford models?' they asked, astonished.

'I'm afraid it's true,' I said now conscious of a lapse.

The girls looked from one to the other in amazement. Then one of them said: 'But couldn't we help?'

'You mean?' I asked, fearing that next moment there was going to be a silver collection.

'Why, we'll come along and pose for you,' she said.

'The time is short,' said their chaperone. 'We have only four days before Paris.'

'But we are free in the afternoons,' said another, tall and fair-haired.

'We'll come three at a time,' said a short brunette.

They were as good as their word. For the rest of that week they came to my studio in threes, and on the last day the whole twelve came together, and not only did they all pose for me but their chaperone did too—thirteen of them, my lucky number. As I looked about my studio that day and saw group after group, as in a classic frieze, I wouldn't have given tuppence for the Elgin Marbles.

CHAPTER TWENTY-SIX

THE PAINTINGS of Chaim Soutine have until a few years ago been known to but a small public, for the artist had not only an inherent dislike of exhibiting his new work but a ruthless intention in destroying any earlier canvases that fell into his hands. Four of his paintings are now in the Girardin Collection at the Petit-Palais.

Born in Lithuania in 1894, the tenth child of poor parents, Soutine had an unhappy childhood. He was scorned and bullied both at home and at school, and in the streets of the ghetto in which he lived he saw little but misery: for him any hint of brighter things could only be the forerunner of further grief. It is this sadness and disillusion that he has expressed in so many of his earlier paintings whether the subject be an ageing actress, choir-boys, or young girls dressed for their first Communion. It was not until he was twenty-five that the opportunity came for him to spend three years in the country in the clear air of the south of France. Then gradually his outlook became transformed, illumined. His mind was released from the soiled cage of narrow streets, and joyous as a bird in love flight it wheeled among the trees and soared among the clouds, dipping and tumbling. Sunlight and the sweet scents of growth had taken the place of shadows and rancid smells.

In 1929 Soutine was one of the fifty artists chosen by the Russian actress, Madame Maria Lani, to paint or sculp her portrait. Among the other forty-nine were Derain, Leger, Lurçat, Chirico, Foujita, Pascin, Picabia, Rouault, Friesz, van Dongen, Valadon, Despiau, Zadkine, Ozenfant, Marquet, Bonnard, Chagall, Kwapil, Laborde, Gromaire, Kisling, Laboureur, Orloff, Dufy: men already famous or soon afterwards to reach fame. We are told that Foujita gave her a feline expression, Pascin that of a little girl; Bonnard saw her as a gentle widow, Kwapil as a soul in torment. Rouault retained of her only a mask, Valadon put her in the lower middle class, Friesz showed her as a serene tragedienne. Variety enough, one might think, yet perhaps not quite sufficient, for did not Paul Poiret, the *couturier,* say of the lady: 'She is everything in turn; she is at once candour and deceit, purity, vice, love, hate, irony, suffering, and lastly woman.'

Where would painting be without human vanity, directly in the portrayal of features or indirectly in the mere fact of possession? As with painting, so with books: *le snobisme* is the greatest patron of fine editions. In the old days at the Golden Cockerel Press I used to joke about it, saying: 'Never mind about misprints, nobody is going to *read* the book.'

With autographs, too: what has the author's signature on the fly-leaf of a printed book to do with what is printed within? Originally, I suppose, it meant that that particular copy had been given to a personal friend; to-day generally, it means that the author has given something for

nothing to a stranger. When any author friend of mine
is about to present me with one of his books, I beg that
he will not sign it. Then it remains a token known only
to ourselves. Inscribed, it can only develop into an 'item'
in a catalogue.

Concerning such items: two strange coincidences in
my own experience. In 1949, when it was decided to re-
issue my *Coconut Island*, a children's tale of the South
Seas, I needed a spare copy for revision, my own having
been lost in the war. The book proved gratifyingly scarce,
and it was only after many inquiries that I received a
quotation from Liverpool, the bookseller adding that as
it was an inscribed copy he would have to charge me a
small premium. When I opened the book I read on the
fly-leaf in my own handwriting, 'To my daughter Brigid,
with love from her father.' As Brigid was living in South
Africa when, on publication in 1936, I sent her the book,
it was all the more surprising. However, though the
coincidence remains, her explanation was simple: 'Oh,
that was Bill So-and-so,' she said; 'I lent it to him in Lady-
smith years ago and he never gave it back.'

Then last year, while I was in Paris, another sugges-
tion for a reprint came to me, this time of my little picture
book *A True Tale of Love in Tonga*. In my reply, I said
that if needed I could produce a copy from my flat in
London. To this there was no response and I presumed
that all that was needed had been found. Months later,
when the proofs came to me and with them the copy from
which the printers had worked, I found inside the cover

not my own autograph but that of my sister who had died
seven years before. My publishers don't remember how
they got hold of that copy—they think it was by chance in
the Charing Cross Road.

I have often wondered why civic authorities, curators
of museums, art galleries, and other places of interest
abroad on whom the duty falls of preparing guidebooks
for visitors from other countries do not think it worth
while to have their words checked and their proofs read
by native-born speakers of the language. Again and again
when travelling in Europe I have found examples of the
most fantastic English in publications which, though designed solely to give information, defeat that intention
through lack of care. How much do we learn of an his-
toric event in the city of Troyes from the following words
in the official guide? 'The city bedecked with oriflammed
and échang the golden cries of trimpt where, formerly,
the princess clothed yellow dress under the heavy ermine
clothe, a crown on her forehead and, pacific sceptre, a
blossomed branch of apple-tree in hand, hat strand the city
prepares.' Even in Paris, at the Louvre, there is a similar
lack of lucidity. Of a picture by Jan Steen entitled *Bad
Company*, the catalogue tells us: 'The goung green horse
who has ventured into a haunt of vice is being rabbed
while in a drunken sleep.' On the other hand, a reference
to the naiads in one of Rubens' pictures, 'with their supple
fat fresh looking plump bodies over which the water is
streaning with drops like pearlss,' does create a richer men-

tal image than might have been achieved with more classical English.

Wondering if on our side of the Channel we order these things better than they do in France, I inquired at the British Museum, the National Gallery, and the Tate Gallery for their catalogues in French. Alas, we don't even think of such things in England.

2 Juillet—17 Octobre, 1954: Hommage à Cézanne. Paintings covering forty years of the artist's life from a self-portrait painted when he was about twenty-two years of age to a still life that he did within a few years of his death at the age of sixty-seven.

The first impression on entering the gallery is that it is the work not of one man but of many, so often did he alter his style, ever dissatisfied, all the time seeking. Some of his early work might belong to the Spanish school, some is influenced by Italian masters. Even at the age of fifty-three when staying with Camille Pissarro at Pontoise he did not hesitate to copy a picture by his friend, that he might learn the principles of its luminous colour. Thus finally did he achieve those monumental qualities which are his own, that style which is as architectural in the laying on of paint as in the building up of design. It is sad to think that living in seclusion at Aix his neighbours thought of him only as a grumpy and stingy old man who perpetrated grotesque paintings, and that he, to whom the richness of feminine beauty meant so much, dare not have a nude model in his studio for fear of local scandal.

CHAPTER TWENTY-SEVEN

OR A LONG WHILE, both in Italy and in France, I had been appreciating not only the flavour of artichokes but the form. There came an afternoon on the Île when, returning from the *alimentation générale*, I put a pair of them on the kitchen table and for later convenience stood a bottle of oil and one of vinegar beside them. They made a pretty group, and a few aluminium pans hanging on the wall behind added to the composition. 'Must paint them in the morning,' I thought; 'bang goes my change of diet—eggs again for supper.' Then it seemed a pity to wait until morning—there would be enough light to get them roughed in on the canvas. Indian red, a quick-drying colour, was already on my palette. I'd begin with that as a monochrome and have fun with the colour next day.

There was still daylight when I had done all that I could with the red. Might as well strike a note of green on the fruit, I thought, and when I had done that, might as well put a touch of blue on the aluminium. Just as the light was going the door-bell rang and I found Mark outside.

'Still working?' he asked.

'Been doing a lay-in for the morning,' I said, leading him to the kitchen door. He looked at the picture awhile, stepped forward to scrutinize it more closely, stepped back to view it from a distance. Then he came to where I was standing and took the palette from my thumb. 'Excuse me,' he said, 'but your painting is finished. You must not touch it again.'

So I had artichokes for supper after all, and their portrait is my frontispiece.

Mark would not stay. He had only dropped in to say that he and Ria had decided to leave Paris for a few weeks and that I must come and see them again on their return. They were going to Fontainebleau, to camp in the forest. He needed the peace of growing things about him. They would sleep in the open, he said: the festival of night was unknown to those who slept indoors. I remarked on the natural sandy paths that one finds everywhere in the forest. 'Trodden by the feet of naiads,' he murmured. 'Sometimes my wife joins them; in the moonlight, with hair unbound, she dances. The sand of the forest is soft to bare feet.'

He had hardly left me when my bell rang again. This time it was a husky young woman with multi-coloured hair whom I had never seen before.

'Is Monsieur Mark the poet here?' she asked, pushing

her way in. She was wearing earrings that looked like the circular tops of cigarette tins, and under a loose, black jacket I saw a purple shirt.

'He was here till a few moments ago,' I said, 'but he has left.'

'But they told me that he *was* here,' she said.

'He *was* here,' I emphasized.

'Where is he now?'

'In Paris,' I said, 'or on his way to Fontainebleau. I don't know which.'

'Fontainebleau?'

'Yes, to camp in the forest.'

'Who is with him?'

'His wife, I think.'

'*Always* his wife!'

She walked across the room and studied herself intently in the big mirror.

'I could have expressed myself in the forest,' she said, 'among the beeches.' She ran her fingers through her hair and then threw her arms wide. 'Great smooth bifurcated limbs,' she mused, 'and the tangle of leaves—like torn lace.'

I hinted to the girl that I was busy, but she showed no inclination to go.

'Those curtains,' she said, turning towards the window, 'what a wonderful dress they would make!'

'They're not mine,' I told her hastily; 'they belong to the studio.'

'But the colour—it's perfect for my skin.' She made

a move in their direction, but I headed her off. Eventually I managed to manœuvre her to the door.

'I will come and see you again,' she said, as she went out. 'We will have lunch together one day.'

'Is your name Bella by any chance?' I asked.

'Oh, how did you know? Did my personality come through?'

'Sometimes I have second-hand sight,' I said.

It may be that I did not leave the artichokes long enough to boil that evening and that they lay heavy on my stomach during the night. Anyway, I slept badly, trying all the time to rescue a chubby child who was picking flowers in the shadow of a falling tree.

Just a month since egg-laying and already the young pigeons were well-feathered and strong enough to be left by themselves in the nest for the greater part of the day. Only at feeding times did the parents put in an appearance. Then on the fifteenth day after they had been hatched a new cycle began. That evening on the same upper branch as before their parents were again billing, caressing, and mating, and that night for the first time the youngsters were left alone. Next day I noticed the cock and hen inspecting the fork of another tree a few yards to the left, and the following morning soon after dawn they began to build there. But this time something went wrong with their plans and after a few days' work they abandoned the site. Then, except when they came to my sill for corn, I saw them only when they fed their nestlings.

It was when the youngsters were just three weeks old that I saw their first venture from the nest—only a few feet along the branches and then back to safety. I reckoned that next day or the day after I might see them fly. But I was wrong. I had to leave the house for a couple of hours that morning, and when I came back they were gone. Whatever hesitations they may have shown at first trusting to their wings, whatever inducement to cast themselves upon the air their parents may have offered, I missed them all. But I saw the young birds many times afterwards, so I knew that they had escaped the river. The parents began yet a third nest, using some of the old material for the building, but the tree they chose was not visible from my window and I was unable to watch their progress.

Another who dropped out of my life at this time was Nicole. She had become so interested in her own painting that she lost interest in mine. She made no attempt to conceal her yawns, and when I asked her if she was tired she said no, that it was her liver. A week later when I expostulated she said it was her fiancé. So I took to painting grape-fruit, red and green peppers, and bananas, which had just as nice shapes and were much less temperamental.

On the morning of the 4th August, a letter dated the 15th April reached me from America. It had been following me about Europe at an even more leisurely pace than my own travelling. George Macy, of the Limited Editions Club of New York, had written to ask if I would do some engravings for a new edition of Darwin's *Voyage of the Beagle*. No escape from engraving, I thought, as I sat down to accept. Of what George Macy was thinking at the precise moment when I was writing to him I have no knowledge, but I do know from subsequent letters that just then, when my musings were upon tropical forests and coral islands, he was sauntering along the Quai de Bourbon under my windows, with as little idea that I was east of the English Channel as I had that he was east of the Atlantic.

At any rate the frontispiece should be easy, I reckoned: a portrait of the old man, with rugged features, bushy white beard, and shining bald head against a dark background. Frontispieces are always a problem, and because of the limitations of the medium most portraits are hell to an engraver on wood. Here it seemed was a sitter in every sense of the word. But some months later when it occurred to me to have a look at the diary from which Darwin's Journal was composed, my image fell to bits. Darwin, it appeared, had once been a young man. I had always thought of him as old and mature from birth. Instead, here he was at the age of twenty-two, with few scientific qualifications, setting out on a journey whose consequences would one day rock not only the foundations of coral islands but those of established Christian beliefs. When Darwin left England he was hardly more than a boy, whose chief interest was partridge shooting and whose future was probably ordination and the life of a country clergyman. When he returned after five years he was a scientist: according to his father, even the shape of his head had altered.

It is ironic that Captain Fitzroy who invited Darwin to accompany him on the *Beagle* did so because, as his granddaughter Lady Barlow has pointed out, he wished to have on board a naturalist who would not only 'collect useful information' but also gather knowledge that would ultimately confute the geological sceptics who impugned the strict and literal truth 'of every statement contained in the Bible.' Fitzroy was a devout believer in the first chapters of Genesis, and his almost fanatical outlook, developing in fervour during the voyage, whilst his messmate was developing a fervour in the scientific research for truth, must have been a strange element in their friendship. Darwin left England in 1831 with unshaken belief in immutability and the creationist point of view; in 1837, less than a year after his return to England, he was completely convinced of the transmutation of species, and had set himself to seek out the laws of change.

Though Darwin suffered terribly from seasickness during the whole voyage, he did not let it affect his intense enthusiasm for every new phenomenon of nature that came before his eyes. His excitement was continuous and unbounded: writing of his first day in a Brazilian forest, he says: 'The delight one experiences in such times bewilders the mind; if the eye attempts to follow the flight of a gaudy butterfly, it is arrested by some strange tree or fruit; if watching an insect one forgets it in the stranger flower it is crawling over; if turning to admire the splen-

dour of the scenery, the individual character of the foreground fixes the attention. The mind is a chaos of delight,
out of which a world of future and more quiet pleasure
will arise.' Of his second day in the forest, he says:
'Delight is a weak term for such transports of pleasure.'
Of his third day: 'To a person fond of natural history
such a day as this brings with it pleasure more acute than
he ever may again experience.' Of his fourth day: 'I can
only add raptures to the former raptures.'

It was at about nine o'clock on the night of the 25th
August that the sound of voices chanting drew me to my
window. Looking down, I saw a glow-worm procession
of lights moving slowly along the quay—men and women,
four and five abreast, each with a lighted candle cupped
in a paper shield. At intervals banners were borne, crimson, white and blue, gold-fringed, some with strange de-
vices. The voices carried by the night wind sounded thin
and plaintive, litanies and responses many times repeated.
A man's voice under my window called: 'St Louis, prie
pour nous,' and those about him repeated his words. A
second and a third time came the same invocation and a
like response. Then three times he prayed, 'St Louis,
sauve la France,' and three times his words were echoed.
The stream of pilgrims seemed endless; it was as if an
unbroken ring of lights and supplications were circling
the island. But finally the priests in their white robes
appeared and with them images of the saint carried high,
amidst flaming torches.

I can't help feeling sorry for St Louis. His mother,

Blanche de Castille, who on the death of his father Louis
VIII assumed the regency, had the highest qualifications
for that office, but she also had a fanatical zeal for the
religious upbringing of her son. From his earliest days
she instilled into him the error of all worldly pleasures,
and when the time came for him to marry it was she who
chose his wife. Not only that but, having made sure that
he spent the first three nights of his married life in solitary
prayer instead of with his bride, she on the fourth night
ensconced herself in a room adjoining the bridal chamber.
Waiting there until to her way of thinking he had had
time to consummate the marriage, she called to him and
ordered him to his own room. His duty was to provide an
heir to the throne of France, not to grow fond of his wife
—that might distract him from the love and obedience
that he owed to his mother. Such was her domination
that in the course of time the Château at Pontoise became
the favourite residence of the young people. There the
royal apartments were one above the other and connected
by a spiral staircase. On that staircase, with the con-
nivance of the court ushers, they would hold converse
together, ready to hurry to their respective chambers at a
signal of the maternal approach.

Of the later life of Louis, his part in the Crusades, his
bringing to Paris the many sacred relics that he bought
at enormous prices from an impecunious but astute Emperor of Constantinople and housed in the Sainte Cha-
pelle, and of the many other acts that he did, I will not
speak, for are they not written in the books of the chro-
nicles of the Kings and Queens of France?

CHAPTER TWENTY-EIGHT

On my last Sunday on the Île another fête was held—*Une Grande Fête Nautique,* with a floating ring for *la boxe, le catch,* and *le judo.* Bands of the 'Guardians of the Peace' assisted. The focal point of the review, with officials on grandstands bright with flags and bunting, was on the mainland, on the northern bank of the river; but that was all to the good for us islanders who, standing or sitting on our own quay or its walls, had an uninterrupted view of what was happening. The festivities had been organized by the proprietors of a well-known aperitif, and the day had begun with a fishing match, the final for the Championship of the World of *la pêche au coup,* fishing with a rod but without a reel. The fisherman strikes at the first nibble and without attempt to 'play' jerks the fish on to the shore. The winner of this international championship had in the space of three hours caught ninety-six fish, whose total weight was just over two pounds—the fish in the Seine are not very large.

The sports part of the programme began at three o'clock in the afternoon with aquatic jousting, heralded by a clamour of martial music, the noises of the brass and drums echoing and re-echoing across the river. Instead of on horses, the knights rode in boats, long canoe-shaped craft each equipped with five pairs of men with paddles and a sloping platform extending beyond the stern on which he of the lance took his stand. One of these boats

was blue and the other red; the blue one had blazoned on its side 'Tiens toi bien,' the red one proclaimed 'Prends garde à toi.' The atmosphere was one of medieval pageantry, with crowds sitting and standing along the quays and bridge as if around a tourney ring. Banners and pennons were flying, and the steeply gabled roofs of the small river-control houses suggested the pavilions of former days.

It was from the Île St-Louis that the contesting boats set out. They paddled quietly to their appointed positions, one above and one below the judges' stand, about a hundred yards apart.

At a whistle of command each jouster leaped to his feet and stood at attention, his twenty-foot wooden lance vertical, while the members of each crew held their paddles upright in salute. But only for a moment. There was a roll of drums and the action was on. Each crew dug deep into the water and the war canoes sped towards the combat. As they came near the one to the other, each champion on his platform dropped his lance to the horizontal, slid one foot forward and the other back, and crouched so low that from the hinder heel to the tip of his lance was one straight line. Then the combatants met, the point of each man's lance stabbing the centre of the shield that the other carried on his left arm. There was a moment's tension, with timbers bending, and then a splash.

A roar of delight went up from the crowd. 'C'est la rouge qui est dans l'eau—c'est la *rouge!*' shrieked a small girl in my ear, as she bounced with joy on her father's shoulders.

The red knight was indeed in the water, his weapon floating beside him. He was quickly rescued and soon the canoes were in position for the second bout. This time the impact was such that both lances snapped under the strain. In the third round it was the blue knight who was unhorsed. From a loud-speaker on the judge's rostrum came the announcement that further contests would be held later.

As the raft that carried the boxing ring was being towed into position, I noticed Jules the photographer on the quay just below me. He was trying to get a picture of the one man in the neighbourhood who was showing no interest in the proceedings—a fisherman sitting amidships in his boat with his rod in one hand and a pipe in the other, dozing the afternoon away.

Le Catch, all-in wrestling, was the next item. Two men, brought to the ringside in a boat, climbed through the ropes and went to opposite corners. One of them, lean and swarthy with black curly hair, was wearing black silk trunks; the other, pink-skinned, nearly bald, and in-

clined to stoutness, preferred red satin. At a signal they
rushed at each other and almost immediately the lighter-
weight dark man was picked up and hurled over the
other's shoulder. He came down on the flat of his back,
and the shock of his fall sent ripples across the river. But
it seemed no shock to him, for he was on his feet in an
instant and into another clinch. It was only a moment
before he was again hurled into the air and further ripples
came towards us. The same thing happened a third time.
Then the man who had been thrown changed his tactics.
Instead of letting himself be drawn close enough for another throw, he ran at his opponent and jumping high,
with his two feet together, kicked him in the chest. This
time both men fell on their backs, and no sooner were
they up than the manœuvre was repeated and down they
went again. That seemed enough of violent action, for
they now went into a clinch in which they tried merely
to dislocate a limb or destroy a feature. But this slow
straining of muscles quickly gave way to a non-stop acrobatic display in which each of the contestants seemed to
inflict the most agonizing damage on the other, kicking
him in the face, butting him in the stomach, almost throt-
tling him, almost blinding him. I noticed that each gave
as good as the other, indeed the offensive actions became
so reciprocal that the affair began to look more like a ritual
dance than a fight. When at the end of it all the referee
held up a hand of each of the fighters in token of mutual
victory, I wondered if perhaps it had not been a 'friendly
match.' When the two gladiators landed at the Quai de

Bourbon, showing not a bruise or even a reddening of the skin, and walked arm in arm to their dressing-room, my suspicions were confirmed.

During the display Jules had joined me on the upper quay. He hoped from where I was standing to get a photograph of the juvenile band on the point of the Île below us. These boys and girls were dressed in white with black cummerbunds or sashes and blue peaked caps piped with scarlet. They had only two tunes in their repertoire, one or other of which they played whenever the police band on the other side of the river fell silent. But the crowd was too thick for the camera to come into action. It seemed that every resident of the island and many visitors as well were now present on that small point of land.

In the boxing that came next on the programme, the men in the ring made no pretences: they wore protective headgear, dispensed with a referee, and gave an entirely delightful demonstration of sparring agility.

The finals of the water jousting followed and the blue knight was adjudged the champion. As in token of victory he threw his lance into the river, a thunder shower dispersed the multitudes, and the pageant ended abruptly.

Jules joined me in a sprint to my studio. 'There's one of your pigeons on the window-sill,' he said, as we went in.

'That's Monsieur,' I said, 'and the time must be about five thirty.'

'Five thirty-five, to be exact,' said Jules, looking at his watch.

Regularly for weeks past, between five and six o'clock

in the evening, that pigeon had come to my window-sill.
Madame had but rarely put in an appearance. As I opened
the window the bird, seeing a stranger in the room, moved
just a little further away. But he came immediately to
the corn that I put down and ate hurriedly. He was looking thin and dishevelled, and the reason was obvious when
his two almost fully grown youngsters arrived and demanded to be fed. Rather than submit to their exactions
he flew away, leaving them to finish the grain.

I was sorry when I had to leave that bird, for I felt that
an understanding had grown up between us. It is difficult
to explain to a dog that one is going away but will some
day come back; it is impossible to explain to a pigeon why
there will be no more corn on the sill. The strange thing
was that on my last day in the studio that bird came to
the window early, and up to the time of my leaving spent
the whole day there. Not only that, but at intervals he
would put his head through the iron railing and peer into
the room, a thing he had never done before.

Meanwhile, with Jules I crossed the river again, passing
at the far end of the bridge an artist at work on a painting
of Notre Dame.

'He was there when I came along at three o'clock,' said
Jules.

'He was there at ten o'clock this morning,' I said, 'when
I came across to get some stamps. What's more, he was
doing the same subject. The sun was behind him then.'

'Perhaps he wants to unite all the effects of the day on
one canvas,' said Jules, 'like the fellows who combine half

the outside of a vase with half its inside, in order to express its entirety.'

At the Métro station in the Place St-Michel Jules said good-bye: he and Madeleine were going to a concert. Left to myself I sat awhile at the Taverne du Palais, watching the variegated multitude of passersby. Africans sauntering, Chinese hurrying, Indians and Burmese with stately gait, Europeans and Americans not so stately. Then, mingling with the crowd, I made my way slowly and contemplatively up the Boul. Mich. On my right I passed the old-established emporium of '100,000 Chemises'; on my left, at the corner of the Place de la Sorbonne, the site of the now extinct Café d'Harcourt. I had a tenderness for that brasserie, for nearly thirty years ago I did a painting there—winding staircase, couple of clients, couple of waiters, and a corner of the orchestra. As ever, book shops on either side of the road spread on to the pavement, their stocks as diverse as the arrangement of subjects was incongruous. It occurred to me then that for many of us life is like a book whose binder has been careless. Sheets have been wrongly folded, or sections misplaced, and so opportunities arrive at the wrong moment, and in the middle of romance we meet sudden tragedy. Or a section has been duplicated, and we find the same pages a second time; then we say, 'History repeats itself.'

From the Boul. Mich. into the Luxembourg Gardens, with the fountains, the chestnut avenues, the nursemaids, and the grey stone queens of other days. There stood

Marie de Medici, proud and haughty, beside Marguerite de Navarre, demure and coy. Strange that such a saintly woman as Marguerite should have written such a book as the *Heptameron*. But then her melancholic brother, Francis I, whom she adored, needed distraction, and such stories as she wrote, based on contemporary anecdotes, served also to emphasize to him some of the weaknesses that had crept into the Church at that period.

And from the Gardens to Montparnasse, with its mass

production of men and women, old and young, carrying portfolios or canvases. Some full of assurance though with nothing accomplished, others diffident though with much to their credit; some cynical after a few failures, others after years of disappointment convinced of ultimate success.

What was it all about, I wondered, as so many others have also wondered—this urge that often is stronger than hunger? A few lines or colours in harmony can give more delight to their creator than a Lucullan feast. There is no need for intellect or erudition, or even of being 'civilized'. As Picasso has said of the cave paintings at Lascaux, some fifteen or twenty thousand years old, 'Nothing finer has since been done.' Then I thought of the sculptures on the Indian temples dating from early centuries B.C., friezes of which each figure is a perfect note in an oft-repeated chord. A prince of India once desired of a sage that he should be taught the principles of art, meaning of painting and of sculpture. 'But you must know first the principles of music and after that the principles of dance,' said the sage, 'for all art is one.'

As I glanced ahead of me, I saw the roseate lights of La Coupole. But even Lucullus, I remembered, dined on occasions *chez* Lucullus. I looked straight to my front till I reached the Gare Montparnasse and then I hopped on to a bus that took me back to the river—my lovely river full of stars.

For the time being my days in Paris were over. A long way round and a short stay at home it had been, for Paris is always home to me. And what was there to show for it all? A few small paintings and perhaps a few words. Well, as I heard it said in Positano, 'An egg to-day is better than a hen to-morrow.' Hatching takes an awful long time.